GOVERNMENT IN SWEDEN

The Executive at Work

BY

NEIL C. M. ELDER, M.A., B.LITT.

Senior Lecturer in Political Studies

University of Hull

PERGAMON PRESS

Oxford · New York · Toronto · Sydney · Braunschweig

Pergamon Press Ltd., Headington Hill Hall, Oxford
Pergamon Press Inc., Maxwell House, Fairview Park, Elmsford, New York 10523
Pergamon of Canada Ltd., 207 Queen's Quay West, Toronto 1
Pergamon Press (Aust.) Pty. Ltd., 19a Boundary Street, Rushcutters Bay, N.S.W. 2011, Australia
Vieweg & Sohn GmbH, Burgplatz 1, Braunschweig

First edition 1970

Library of Congress Catalog Card No. 79-110411

Printed in Great Britain by A. Wheaton & Co., Exeter

08 015533 2 (flexicover)
08 015534 0 (hard cover)

TO MY FATHER AND MOTHER

Contents

Foreword

In recent years several introductory studies of government and politics in a number of western European countries have been published. Most of these aim, in different ways, to provide an overview of the political systems of the countries concerned, embracing the organization and behaviour of political parties, the institutional framework of political action, the structure of executive government, and perhaps even the legal system. This new series on government in western Europe, to which Mr. Elder's careful analysis of government in Sweden is the second contribution, has a more specific and restricted purpose. The aim is to concentrate attention on the executive area of government, on how governments are structured, what they do and how they do it, and on their place in the wider political system. Whilst most attention will be given to central government, other levels of public authority will be considered according to their importance in the overall pattern of executive action in the countries dealt with. This approach means that several significant aspects of the political systems in question will have to be left out of account, but it is hoped that this limitation of range will be fully compensated for by the deeper penetration of the executive and administrative areas of activity which it permits. In an epoch in which public authorities everywhere have an increasingly decisive role at all levels as instruments of social engineering, there are surely many reasons for directing the spotlight onto them.

Mr. Elder's volume is to be followed by studies of Spain and West Germany. It is intended that gradually the series should embrace the other countries of western Europe. In this way students of comparative government will eventually have at their disposal a picture of executive government in its various forms in western Europe which, it is hoped, will provide a useful basis for comparative analysis.

University of Warwick NEVIL JOHNSON

Preface

I AM glad to acknowledge a particular debt of gratitude first to Professor W. J. M. Mackenzie, of the University of Glasgow, who kindled my interest in Swedish government and politics when I was at the University of Oxford; second, to Professor C. A. Hessler, Professor of Political Science at the University of Uppsala, who gave me full access to the resources of the Skytteanska Institute (not least the Press archives) during the long hot summer of 1965, when much of the basic work on this small book was done; third, to the Swedish Institute, who—not for the first time—helped me *inter alia* with research materials and much cheerfulness; and fourth, to Queen's College, Dundee, in the University of St. Andrews (as it then was), through whom I obtained a travel grant towards my research expenses while on the lecturing staff. I am also grateful to Professor Nils Andrén, now of the University of Copenhagen; to fil. lic. J.-Å. Wickléus, for kind permission to draw upon an unpublished essay; to Dr. Nils Elvander and to many other Swedish friends and acquaintances for information and advice; to George Dawson, Lecturer in Scandinavian government at the London School of Economics and Political Science, for help with the manuscript; to Mrs. E. B. Gibson, of Hull, and to the late Mrs. K. Hutchings, of Dundee, for help with the typing. The pains of writing have been greatly lightened by my wife, to whom my debt is immeasurable.

Swedish government has been in process of much change of late. Although the basic research for this study was done, as mentioned, in 1965, I have sought to keep up to date in all essentials. No doubt some of the information given here will be overtaken by events before the date of publication. Nevertheless, it is hoped that what is said herein will remain largely relevant and readable. For any errors and possible strange nuances I remain solely responsible.

CHAPTER 1

Introductory

THE place of Sweden on the list of stable democracies is as assured as that of any country can be. She has now been a fully fledged parliamentary democracy for half a century; all parties accept the parliamentary system; the parliamentary system has proved, on the whole, remarkably efficient at adapting to social and economic change and at providing for social and economic needs; and governments have been quite remarkably stable. This last circumstance could, of course, itself be a source of instability, but a number of factors have operated to prevent the opposition groups from becoming estranged from the system: it is hoped to throw some light on these factors in what follows.

The pace of political, social, and economic change in Sweden in the years preceding the emergence of modern parliamentary democracy was surprisingly rapid and generated a good deal of friction, but it did not lead to instability. Much is often made of the homogeneity of Swedish society as a factor in the general stability, and it is true, for example, that there are no politically significant national minorities and that well over 90 per cent of the population officially belongs to the Lutheran Church. Nevertheless, it seems fair to make the point that it is possible to over-concentrate on this factor: for example, only some 3 per cent of the population attends Sunday morning Lutheran services today,[1] and social cleavages in the years preceding the appearance of a modern parliamentary democracy were quite sharp and distinct. The importance of political

[1] Anna-Lisa Kälvesten, *The Social Structure of Sweden*, Swedish Institute, Stockholm, 1965, p. 67.

circumstance, and of political sagacity in adapting to change, has been considerable.

Not until 1866 did the ancient legislature of the four estates disappear: the houses of the Nobility, Clergy, Burghers, and Peasants voted themselves off the political scene, to be replaced by a bicameral Riksdag. The estates had, it is true, already become an anachronism, but, even so, three-quarters of the population at the time still depended for a living on agriculture, and the industrial revolution was still in its infancy. The reorganization of Parliament made possible the emergence of more coherent parliamentary parties, but these rested on a narrow social base on account of the highly restrictive property franchise. Political power was shared between higher civil servants, landed aristocrats, propertied farmers, and merchants, only now on somewhat more favourable terms for the latter groups.

Between 1866 and 1910 industrialization and the growth of commerce proceeded apace. By the latter year about a third of the population depended on industry for its livelihood, while the corresponding figure for agriculture fell to just under a half. Conditions were thus created favourable to the development of mass political movements, and a large migration of population naturally occurred into the towns and cities, although the scale of individual industrial enterprises remained on the whole comparatively small. In 1889, August Palm founded the Social Democratic Workers' Party on the basis of the Gotha Programme of the German Social Democrats. At about the same time Free Church, temperance, student, and other organizations were beginning to appear with strong support among the intelligentsia, the artisans, and the lower middle class and to campaign along Radical–Liberal lines in favour of electoral reform.[2] (Official Free Church membership, it may be added, has remained well under 10 per cent of the total number of persons registered as belonging to a religious denomination, but the Free Churches have exercised a political influence out of proportion to their numbers—and their numbers were, in any case, always weightier than the

[2] These movements preceded the formation of the Liberal Union Party—the forerunner of the modern Liberal Party.

figures indicate, because many did not officially secede from the State Church.)

In this situation, Liberals and Social Democrats soon made common cause on the question of electoral reform, and after some tactical differences agreed in 1902 to press for universal suffrage. In 1907–9 universal manhood suffrage was conceded in the course of a compromise settlement with the forces of conservatism:[3] the *quid pro quo* was the introduction of a proportional representation electoral system designed to preserve the position of minority groups. In 1913 the first Farmers' Party made its appearance; in 1917–18 the principle of parliamentary cabinet government finally triumphed, the end of the monarchy as an independent political force was achieved, and the franchise was extended to the entire adult population.

THE ERA OF SOCIAL DEMOCRATIC ASCENDANCY: INTRODUCTORY

Government in Sweden has now been dominated by one party for more than a generation. That party—the Social Democratic Labour Party—to give it its full name—emerged as the largest single party in the Lower House of the Swedish Parliament in 1914 and reached a similar position in the Upper House a few years later. It has been in office continuously from 1932, with the exception of a hundred days in 1936. Certainly it has not had a monopoly of power during these years of office. It came back from the wilderness in 1932 as a minority government (after three short spells of minority government in the 1920's). From 1933 until shortly after the outbreak of the Second World War it depended much on support from the Farmers' (now the Centre) Party: from 1936 to 1939 it was the major party in a so-called Red–Green coalition. During the war years it headed an emergency coalition of all the four major parties of the country—Social Democrats, Farmers, Liberals, and Conservatives. (The Conservatives have just, in January 1969, renamed themselves the Moderate Alliance Party—*Moderata Samlingspartiet*—but the old name will be retained in this book as being that by which

[3] The forerunner of the modern Moderate Alliance (Conservative) Party dates from 1904—the General Voters' Alliance.

they were known at the time.) From 1951 to 1957 the Social Democratic Party again ruled in coalition with the Farmers' Party, losing a majority in the Lower House when its ally retired into opposition in the latter year. From 1958 to 1968 it owed much in divisions to steady support from the small Communist Party (now the Communist Left Party). But despite all these qualifications the fact remains that the Social Democrats have been the principal force active on the Swedish political scene for the past 37 years. The party has been not far off an absolute majority in the Lower House of the Riksdag since 1936—it achieved such a majority, indeed, between 1940 and 1944, and again, most recently, in 1968 and it was as strong there as all the other parties combined between 1944 and 1948. It has, moreover, had an absolute majority in the Upper House since 1942, and this has stood it in good stead in the joint cameral votes by which finance questions have been decided. It has, finally, given Sweden the only two prime ministers she has had since 1932 if the short interval in the summer of 1936 be again left out of the reckoning.[4]

This long spell of virtually unbroken rule is in part, but only in part, to be explained in terms of the changes that have been taking place in the social structure of the country. The most significant fact here has, of course, been the growth of the industrial working class. The proportion of the population directly dependent on industry for its livelihood has doubled since the turn of the century until it is now not far off a half of the total. The proportion living off the land—counting forestry and fisheries under that head—has fallen over the same period from above a half to less than a sixth of the total. The remainder, who are an expanding category both in absolute and relative numbers, are connected with service trades, public employment, etc., and include a large proportion of salaried employees. Between two-thirds and three-quarters of the total working-class vote has been going to the Social Democrats.[5]

[4] Prime Minister Erlander retired in September 1969, so that the total is now three.

[5] For voting figures, see Nils Stjernquist, Sweden, Stability or deadlock?, in R. A. Dahl, *Political Oppositions in Western Democracies*, Yale UP, 1966, p. 127.

The Swedish Communist Left Party may also be taken into account in this connection, although it suffered heavily in the 1968 elections. It is a typical Communist Party in that it has a more purely working-class character than any of the other parties, although there have been plenty of signs of late that it is attempting to broaden its appeal. In general elections since 1945 it has polled between 3 per cent and 6 per cent of the total vote and has returned between three and eight members to the Lower House of the Swedish Parliament. These numbers are small, but until 1968 they provided a valuable (though unsolicited) addition to Social Democratic strength in that chamber. They also help to justify the observation that the centre of gravity of the Swedish electorate has been well to the left throughout the post-war period when compared, for example, with that of the British electorate: Social Democrats and Communists together have polled more votes than the three other Swedish parties combined in five out of the seven post-war general elections, and they have reached over 49 per cent of the poll between them in the remaining two elections (1956 and 1958). The Communists, despite various tactical shifts and a change of leadership in 1964, have so far steadily taken the line that a Social Democratic government is preferable to any alternative. With their support the Social Democrats were able virtually to dispose of an absolute majority in the Lower House from 1944 to 1951 and again from 1960 to 1968, while between 1958 and 1960 the two left-wing parties were in effect equal in strength in that chamber to the three other parties combined.

The Social Democrats could not have done so well without considerable success in attracting middle-class votes. At their peak performance in the elections of 1940, when they were given an absolute majority of all the votes cast and came back with an absolute majority of the seats in the Lower House, they polled more middle-class votes than any of the so-called bourgeois parties taken singly. This, like the 1944 election, was admittedly an exceptional election: it took place in conditions of national emergency and muted party rivalry. But in the general elections that have taken place since the disintegration of the national coalition in 1945 the Social Democrats have still been able on occasion to rival their strongest single contender in the winning of middle-class support. In consequence they have averaged roughly 46·6 per cent of the total poll at general elections over this period, falling to their lowest point at 44·6 per cent in 1956 and reaching a peak of 50·1 per cent in 1968. In the 1968 elections they gained votes from the Communist Left. Nevertheless, the general unity of swing over the country reflects the cross-class basis of Social Democratic support. The use of proportional representation in the Swedish electoral system has not had the effect of narrowing the appeal of any of the major parties to a limited sectarian base. The Social Democrats have consistently competed for the middle ground: the other course, which is more characteristic of ideological politics, would have run the risk of tilting the balance against them by drawing the splintered opposition closer together.

Social democracy in Sweden has a record of political pragmatism which has long bleached the party's original redness. Its Marxist revolutionary heritage soon disappeared for all practical purposes under the pressure of events. Even before the turn of the century, as was mentioned above, Social Democrats were collaborating with Liberal groups in a campaign for the widening of the franchise. The success of that campaign, at a time when industrialization was going ahead at a rapid pace—in the early years of this century—ensured that the majority within the party would be political moderates seeking reform through parliamentary action. The heavy loss of dues-paying members which followed the general strike of 1909 reinforced the trend. Overt nationalization programmes, again, have played virtually no part in the party's electoral campaigns. A commission of inquiry was appointed on the subject of nationalization in 1920 and sat for 16 years without tangible result. The issue was raised in the party's 1944 post-war programme, but in rather general terms—there was no question of a "shopping list". It awakened sharp partisan controversy and helped break up the national coalition. But when the Social Democrats took office alone in 1945 little more was heard of the matter: the ensuing silence may be contrasted with the internal strife which the question aroused in the British

Labour Party in the 1950's. It would, however, be mistaken to conclude that because the Social Democrats are a party of relatively low doctrinal content, they are therefore essentially a party of astute temporization. They have shown considerable energy in pressing ahead with large-scale extensions to the social services, financed in part by heavy redistributive taxation; they have proved themselves to be very much the party of national planning and they have worked closely with industrial and commercial leaders in the field of economic planning; they have pursued the traditional neutralist–humanitarian line in foreign affairs. All this, combined with a high level of general prosperity for many years (a comparatively sticky economic patch of 2 years or so showed clear signs of coming to an end in the third quarter of 1968), has enabled the party to maintain its attractiveness for a sizeable segment of middle-class opinion. Of late there have been symptoms of renewed radicalization, especially among the younger party members. This tendency has found some reflection in official party policy, for example in the setting up of an investment credit bank, in a revival of interest in the creation of state companies, and, more particularly, in an investigation into the question of industrial democracy. The party leadership has been at some pains in all this to stress its preoccupation with national co-operation and to repudiate the concept of class war.

The Social Democrats owe something of their success to the disunity of the parties to their right.[6] It is not easy to determine the precise influence of this factor, but a number of considerations are relevant. Firstly, the Social Democrats have managed to enlist the support of the Farmers' Party—now the Centre Party—on tactically important occasions. Secondly, the very success of the Social Democrats has at times had the effect of disheartening the opposition somewhat. Thirdly, there is the question of whether or not the three main minority parties could unite on terms that would save them from a permanent minority position.

[6] See Bo Särlvik, Political stability and change in the Swedish electorate, *Scandinavian Political Studies* **1** (1966), 188–222, for a detailed analysis from another angle of the phenomenon of the long Social Democratic ascendancy.

The Role of the Farmers' (Centre) Party

The Social Democrats paved the way for their ascendancy when they concluded the 1933 "horse-trading" agreement with the Farmers' Party on the basis of a programme of reflationary anti-depression measures in general and of aid to primary producers in particular. The success of this programme was reflected in success for the Social Democrats at the polls in 1936, and this in turn stimulated the formation of the first Red–Green coalition during whose tenure the Social Democrats began their large-scale reforms on the welfare front.

The detachment of the Farmers' Party from the opposition thus gave the Social Democrats a valuable accession of strength and their first taste of real power. The same manœuvre was successfully repeated in the post-war years, although this time it took longer to achieve. The first approach was made by the Social Democrats in 1948 after the general election of that year had revealed a falling-off in popular support for them (the approach itself revealed the lack of affection with which the party regarded Communist support). The result was negative. The electoral laws which were then in force put a premium upon the formation of cartels, and the Farmers' Party feared the results of electoral isolation from the Liberals and Conservatives. They therefore proposed the formation of a national coalition of the four major parties, and this the Social Democrats were not prepared to countenance. However, a second series of negotiations in 1951 resolved the difficulty, with the result that the electoral system was revised and cartels were prohibited shortly after the second Red–Green coalition took office.

The coalition of 1951–7 helped to tide the Social Democrats over an awkward period during which their strength at the polls continued to ebb. By 1956 the process of decline had reached the point at which they had 13 fewer seats in the Lower House than the three bourgeois parties—too great a deficiency for Communist support to have made good. The decline has been attributed in part to the unpopularity of the coalition, but this would not appear to have weighed very heavily against the Social Democrats in view of the fact that the party's vote remained virtually unaltered at the 1958 elections after the coalition had disintegrated. It was the Farmers'

Party which suffered from the alliance. Electoral revision could not protect them from harm in the absence of votes, and the loss of votes was beginning to assume catastrophic proportions by 1956. After the elections of that year they could only command 19 seats in the Lower House as compared with 30 in 1948. In these circumstances the coalition came under increasing strain until the Farmers' Party eventually withdrew from it in 1957.

The alliance which the Social Democrats had secured with the Farmers' Party thus split the three major opposition groups at a time when the latter in combination could have commanded a parliamentary majority. Towards the end of the life of the coalition the Social Democrats sponsored a scheme for compulsory supplementary pensions with which the Farmers' Party found itself in disagreement. The Conservatives and Liberals managed to agree on a common line in opposition to the scheme and hoped that the Farmers' Party would give them support. They were disappointed: the Farmers' Party, being still in the coalition, struck out on a line of its own. It was at this time—1957—that that party renamed itself the Centre Party, a title which reflected not only its desire to broaden the basis of its support but also its state of mind for some years past.

When the coalition broke down, the Centre Party stuck to its independent line on the pensions question for a time in the hope that this would bring it electoral profit and rejected an offer to enter a new government in alliance with the Liberals and Conservatives. The Social Democrats were thus enabled to carry on alone in a minority position until, in 1958, they were defeated in the Riksdag on the pensions issue by a combination of all three parties against them. But the combination was purely negative, and on the ensuing dissolution of Parliament the three main opposition groups fought separate campaigns. As a result of the election the bourgeois parties collectively suffered a reverse, losing their absolute majority in the Lower House over the left.[7] Both the Centre Party and the Con-

[7] Centre, Liberals, and Conservatives together still obtained just over 50 per cent of the votes cast; the Social Democrats polled much the same as in 1956 but won a higher percentage of the votes cast because of a drop in turnout (they also gained seats by Communist abstentions).

servatives, however, registered gains, and this encouraged them to stand together on a right-wing line on the pensions issue, thereby stranding the Liberals further to the left. Thus both parties, for example, threatened to overturn the pensions act which the Social Democrats eventually put through in 1959, while the Liberals at this point went along with the Government. At the end of this complicated episode[8] the electorate, in 1960, gave the Social Democrats their highest ever peace-time vote until that date, and with it a majority over the Centre Party, Liberals, and Conservatives together, although Communist support was still necessary to ensure a Social Democratic victory in divisions in the Lower House.

It can hardly be said in the light of these events that the Centre Party found any immediate cause to regret the abandonment of electoral cartels once it had broken its association with the Social Democrats. The evidence suggests rather that it enjoyed the pursuit of an independent line. Initially (on the pensions issue) it allied with the Conservatives; at intervals it kept open a channel of communication with the Social Democrats; and on the whole it has been the coolest of the three opposition parties towards the idea of a tripartite coalition. This last point was illustrated, for example, by its brisk disavowal of the candidate of the Citizens' League who applied to it for parliamentary affiliation after winning a seat in the Malmö area in 1964 on the League's platform of a general anti-socialist alliance between Centrists, Conservatives, and Liberals. For the last two or three years before the 1968 election, however, the Centre Party was more and more settling down to an alliance with the Liberals in a determined attempt to dominate the middle ground. Since the election there has been some cooling-off on this front.[9]

It was remarked earlier that the very success of the Social Democrats has had the effect of somewhat disheartening the opposition on occasion. As one would expect, the signs of despondency have generally waxed and waned in proportion to Social Democratic electoral fortunes. Thus the immediate post-war years (1945–8)

[8] An interesting analysis is given by Björn Molin, Swedish party politics: a case study, in *Scandinavian Political Studies* **1** (1966), 45–58.

[9] See below, p. 15.

represented a bad patch for the opposition parties, and so did the first half of the 1960's. During these periods Liberals and Conservative party leaders in particular were to be found attacking despondency in the ranks, and electoral propaganda was at times in a decidedly minor key—witness, for example, the 1964 election slogan: "To strengthen the opposition, vote Liberal." Since 1965 there has been evidence of a considerable change in the atmosphere, for reasons shortly to be explained. The 1968 election has been something of an exception to the general rule and has not seriously affected opposition morale.[10]

The Idea of a National Coalition

At this point a brief look may be taken at a side-issue that has occasionally come up on the Swedish political scene—advocacy of a permanent national coalition. A feeling of near-despair was discernible at times in the writings of commentators of Conservative or Liberal leanings in face of the apparently inexorable advance of the Social Democrats to power. In Sweden, as elsewhere, fears were expressed that the progress of industrialization would lead to the emergence of a permanent single-party majority. These fears were sometimes conjoined with sympathy towards an older strand in Swedish political tradition, a strand personified by the nineteenth-century liberal patrician Louis de Geer. This school of thought expressed suspicion of classical parliamentarism and the "swing of the pendulum" associated with it. Public business, the argument runs, should be transacted in a spirit of cool objectivity with the minimum of partisanship and the co-operation of all. Opposition groups should seek to exert an influence on public affairs commensurate with their strength rather than act in between elections with the overriding aim of getting the Government out at the first opportunity. Reforms can thus proceed with the maximum rationality and in a quiet and steady flow. Progress will, so to speak, be in a straight line, whereas under a "swing of the pendulum" system it is subject to sharp tacks and changes of direction. The logical end of this line of approach is advocacy of a permanent coalition of all the major currents of

[10] See below, pp. 14–15.

opinion in the country. Such an arrangement, it has been urged,[11] satisfies the crucial condition of a parliamentary system—that the Government shall enjoy the confidence of Parliament. It has been defended as being the fairest way to run the Government in Swedish circumstances and also the most efficient, since it permits maximum use of the talents available and ends the frustrations of perpetual opposition.

Hopes of a permanent four-party coalition as a practicable political proposition were raised by the fact that the Social Democratic premier in the war-time coalition, Per-Albin Hansson, expressed considerable sympathy with the idea. The break-up of that coalition in 1945 was viewed with regret by a number in the ranks of opposition. Thus Professor Elis Håstad, a prominent Conservative politician (and a breezy political fighter when the occasion demanded), campaigned vigorously during the post-war years for a Swiss-type executive and for decisive referenda. The coalition concept had its champions within the Liberal Party too, and even the Centre was, as already mentioned, not unwilling to revive a general coalition in reply to the Social Democratic offer of alliance in 1948, though special circumstances were present in this last case. Sometimes the defence of coalition reflected regret at the passing of the inter-party *camaraderie* of the war-time regime; sometimes it represented a genuine idealism; sometimes it had a tincture of the "if you can't beat 'em, join 'em" philosophy. Whatever the motivation, less has been heard of the idea since post-war Social Democrats have proved themselves stony ground for its reception, since the vote of the salariat has entered increasingly into political calculations and since the hopes of the opposition have revived.

The Opposition Situation and Recent Political Developments

Pessimism was at its strongest of recent years in the ranks of the opposition in the wake of the Social Democratic victory in the

[11] C. A. Hessler, Parlamentarismens begrepp, in *Studier tillägnade Fredrik Lagerroth*, Lund, 1950, pp. 172–82, surveys the main adherents of this line of argument.

general election of 1960. Some read in the events of the previous 4 years the lesson that unification of the three major opposition parties alone could set a term to continued Social Democratic successes. It was under the influence of this belief that a Citizens' League, representative of local sympathizers with all three parties but without central backing, contested the constituency centring on the southern city of Malmö in the 1964 elections and emerged with three seats: it did not succeed in denting Social Democratic strength in the area. More recently a Progressive Union (*Samling för framsteg*) has been formed to campaign for the same general cause; and more recently still, in November 1968, this has been followed (but not, it would seem, superseded) by a new Progressive Party. None of these organizations has at the moment much political force.

Others, again, read the election result of 1960 as implying primarily a judgement on the Conservative Party for setting itself so resolutely against the Social Democratic Pensions Act of 1959. From this point of view, a general unification of the bourgeois parties could only result in a permanent minority position for them while the combination was tarnished by what appeared to many electors to be Conservative hostility to the principles of the welfare State.[12] The polarization of political life on these terms would result, it was feared, in the defection of many Centre Party and Liberal voters to the left. It might be added that, if this were true, the substitution of a majority electoral system for proportional representation would make no difference to the prospect of an indefinite run of Social Democratic successes except through one of those freak results to which a majority system is liable.

The leaders of both the Liberal and Centre parties have on the whole tended of late to follow the second general line of argument. Before the 1968 elections, as mentioned above, they increasingly concerted their actions and policies. The Conservatives, who had

[12] The Conservatives accepted the Pensions Act after the 1960 elections, and much of their opposition to it had in any event been tactical. But subsequent attacks on the size and use of the Pensions Fund established under the Act exposed the Conservatives to this charge again—as did their general approach to taxation policy.

been pressing hard for a tripartite working arrangement, were in consequence left out on a limb. All the parties in opposition had been greatly heartened by the fact that the Labour Government fell in Norway in 1965 after an almost unbroken run of 30 years in office. The Swedish local elections of September 1966 reduced the Social Democratic share of the poll to 42·3 per cent (as compared with 50·5 per cent in the corresponding elections of 1962). The bourgeois parties received a higher share of the poll than the Social Democrats and Communists combined—if, that is, the 1·8 per cent of the votes cast for the new Christian Democratic League, a party with strong support from the small fundamentalist Pentecostal Church, are counted in. In the light of these events, the Centre Party and the Liberals concentrated on making the running on the opposition side, hoping to carry the Conservatives along with them: despite an early truce in inter-party hostilities in the opposition ranks before the 1968 elections and an early tripartite onslaught on government economic policies, neither the Centre Party nor the Liberals hesitated on occasion to make sharp attacks on aspects of Conservative policy—and, in particular, on the Conservative hope of securing extensive tax reductions. This pressure induced the Conservatives to modify their line on one or two issues, including taxation policy. Just before the elections, the two former parties demanded Conservative adherence to their programme as the price of participation in any future government. The general centre of gravity of the post-war Swedish electorate, it was remarked earlier, has been comparatively far to the left. The same holds good within the ranks of the opposition—at least in the sense that the genuinely conservative element is comparatively weak when the other two parties are taken into account.

From the opposition point of view, the 1968 election was certainly a sharp disappointment. The Social Democrats got 125 seats, a gain of 12; the Centre Party 39 (plus 4); the Liberals 34 (minus 9); the Conservatives 32 (minus 1); the Communist Left 3 (minus 5); and the Citizens' League lost its only seat. Fresh elections are to occur to a new unicameral legislature in September 1970, however,[13]

[13] See below, pp. 27–28.

and the opposition parties are buoyed up by the prospect of renewed battle in so short a time. Meanwhile their mutual differences continue along much the same lines as before. The Conservatives (Moderate Alliance) continue to try for a tripartite working agreement and to meet with the same coolness. The pre-election alliance between the Liberals and the Centre Party has faded, as was said, but these two parties are closer to each other than to the Conservatives, and may well revive their earlier tactic.

Why are the Conservatives so comparatively weak in Sweden? Historically they were strongest when the franchise was limited: their strength then lay in the higher civil service, the managerial class, and a section of the farming population. They continue to be a chiefly upper-income-bracket party, stronger now in the towns than the country, and with some small support from workers at lower wage levels. In the countryside they have long had to face stiff competition from a specialist agrarian party. More generally they have often found themselves in the position of resisting the extension of state activity when such an extension has been widely popular. Finally, there is the point that in Sweden today there is no very obvious social elite.

The differences between the Social Democrats and the parties to their right have certainly narrowed over the years. The Liberals have been quick to point out that the Social Democrats have adopted some of the programmes of social liberalism.[14] The growth of farmers' co-operative movements at a time of depression disposed the old Farmers' Party to be sympathetic to programmes of government activism on the economic front. The Conservatives, despite occasional sallies, have in fact abandoned much of their earlier hostility to state welfare programmes. Clearly, the greater the degree of consensus the blunter the cutting edge of opposition. But, as was noted earlier, there are indications that the area of political strife between Government and opposition has been widening again over the past few years. Thus a long period of comparative harmony in the field of defence policy was broken in autumn 1966

[14] As, for example, Bertil Ohlin, *Liberal utmaning*, Bokförlaget Folk och Samhälle, 3rd edn., Arboga, 1963, p. 7.

when the Social Democrats introduced considerable cuts in defence expenditure: these were opposed by all three main opposition parties but the Conservatives, predictably, went furthest in their opposition while the other two agreed on a middle line. The signs of a shift in public opinion at about the same time helped to raise the political temperature: these coincided with a worsening of the country's economic situation and owed much to temporary rising unemployment and to a housing shortage aggravated by credit difficulties. Economic difficulties in their turn evoked fresh government interventions of a controversial character, the most notable perhaps being the imposition of a 25 per cent investment tax on low priority building and the creation of a state-controlled investment credit bank. Both of these measures attracted the hostility of Centre Party, Liberals, and Conservatives alike, but the Conservatives were again alone in rejecting the investment credit bank scheme outright while the other two once more concerted a middle line. In the third quarter of 1968, as was seen, the economic situation improved, but the revived strain of radicalism in the Social Democratic Party seems likely to contribute towards a comparatively high political temperature by Swedish standards, at least till after the 1970 elections.

A Note on the Communist Left Party

A brief look may now be taken at the far left of the political spectrum. Communist strength increased markedly at the 1966 local elections—to 6·4 per cent of the total votes cast as compared with 3·8 per cent in the local elections of 1962. The replacement of Hilding Hagberg, an old-school Stalinist, by C. H. Hermansson as party leader in 1964 brought with it a much more sophisticated style and helped to widen the basis of the party's appeal. The national and local voting age was lowered to 20 in 1966 and the party campaigned vigorously and with a fair measure of success for these new voters, using university students as campaigners and young candidates for many contests. Hermansson was clearly seeking to capture radical support of the type that has given rise to splinter left-wing parties elsewhere in Scandinavia. It is significant in this connection that a number of the candidates standing on the party ticket in 1966 were not themselves party members. It is also significant that in spring 1967 the party changed its name to the Communist Left Party (*Vänsterpartiet kommunisterna*). Hermansson himself was an admirer of Togliatti and has gone further than any other western Communist leader in professing adherence to the rules of the parliamentary game—even to the extent of allowing the possibility of a bourgeois return to power through the polls under a "socialist" regime. None of all this, however, induced the Social Democrats to lend an ear to Communist suggestions that the left should co-operate against the bourgeois parties in the general election of 1968.[15] In the event, schismatic tendencies (a Maoist faction) checked the progress of the Communist Left Party, and the Russian *coup* in Czechoslovakia likewise did nothing to advance its cause—despite the fact that the party leadership vehemently dissociated itself from this operation. Since the 1968 election the party has faded into the background of the political scene.

Summing up thus far, the view which was expressed earlier that the long tenure of office by the Social Democrats owes something to the disunity of the parties to the right rests partly on the earlier behaviour of the Centre Party and partly on the inability of all three opposition parties to co-ordinate their efforts. It does not imply that the unification of the opposition is necessary before a change of regime can occur. Unification is something of an academic question in the present political situation. The position has been tersely expressed by the former Liberal leader, Professor Bertil Ohlin:[16]

> Whatever view one may have about the advantages of party mergers, one has still to remember that these cannot be put through as easily as businessmen amalgamate firms. Parties have grown up as historically conditioned popular movements and they unite people who feel mutually

---

[15] The formation in April 1967 of a Socialist Union represents a Communist attempt to woo the younger Social Democrats to a programme of co-operation at the 1968 polls. It has been repudiated by the Social Democratic leaders.

[16] He was succeeded as leader in 1967 by Sven Wedén.

> connected by common ideas and goals. For the next few years both those who believe that rapid mergers would increase the fighting power of the opposition and those who believe that, on the contrary, mergers under present circumstances would be harmful have no other course but to fight the Social Democratic monopoly of power under conditions which are predetermined as far as the structure of the opposition is concerned.[17]

This was written in 1963 and since then, as was said above, the Liberals and the Centre Party have experimented with concerting their programmes and tactics. But there is no sign as yet that either is willing to compromise its independence.

The Influence of the Electoral System

The introduction of a proportional representation electoral system in 1907–9 has been a factor in the shaping of the Swedish party system. It has tended, as elsewhere, to increase the number of parties, facilitating, for example, the creation of the Farmers' Party which was formed in 1921 by the fusion of two agrarian groups themselves dating from 1913 and 1915. The strengthening of the proportional representation principle in 1921 contributed to the confusion on the parliamentary scene in the next 11 years.[18] During this period six parties were active in politics; each was jealous of its independence of action; a succession of weak minority governments held office, and public policy was shaped more effectively in the committee rooms of the Riksdag than in the Cabinet of the day. The rise of the Social Democrats eventually ended this era, and since then proportional representation has had the usual effect of cushioning the system against more violent oscillations. Although the multiparty pattern has flourished under proportional representation, there is no guarantee that a rapid polarization would occur if a majority system were to be introduced. The Commission on the Constitution, considering this question as a part of its wider remit in its 1963 report, was certain that a change of system would powerfully affect the

[17] Bertil Ohlin, *op. cit.*, p. 13. Ohlin led the Liberals from 1944 to 1967.

[18] A good analysis of the impact of proportional representation in Sweden will be found in Dankwart A. Rustow, *The Politics of Compromise*, Princeton Univ. Press, 1955, pp. 72–76.

existing parties but (not surprisingly) unclear as to what the precise effects would be. Nevertheless, the fact that all the parties have their own distinct ecology, and all have areas of relatively concentrated strength, implies a good short-term chance of survival for them all under a majority system.[19] Not, however, that a change of system is in prospect: the Commission showed some sympathy with the majority system but in the end came down in favour of retaining the principle of proportionality, and subsequent inter-party negotiations have confirmed this. "On the whole it should be considered repugnant to Swedish traditions completely to deprive relatively strong currents of minority opinion of representation over large areas",[20] said the Commission. After a review of the pros and cons of change, the Commission concluded this section of this report by observing that

> it has been clear . . . from the first that a step of this kind should not be taken without the support of a strong and widespread current of opinion manifested within several parties. . . . It is hard to maintain that the criticism of the existing system which has . . . appeared has expressed any widespread dissatisfaction . . . the state of opinion within the parties appears to be unpropitious for the transition to a majority system.[21]

Opposition Influence and Opposition Impotence

It will be evident from what has been said that Sweden has had strong and stable government for many years. The power of government is made more tolerable for opposition groups by a number of factors which help to engage their energies in a positive way, to moderate the spirit of partisanship, and to encourage inter-party compromise. At the local level, the government of communes and many other local authority units, and the administration of some specialized services, is carried out on a proportional representation basis. Local and regional issues, moreover, arise from time to time at the parliamentary level to cross-cut party lines. It is perhaps worth

[19] On the regional distribution of party strengths, see Rustow, *op. cit.*, pp. 134–7.

[20] Statens Offentliga Utredningar, 1963: 17, p. 68.

[21] *Ibid.*, p. 70.

mentioning here that the physical layout of the Swedish Parliament is unusual in that the members—some two-fifths of whom have had local government experience—are seated in their semicircular chambers not by party but by province. Again, the preparation of reforms at the central government level is entrusted on an unusually large scale to commissions of inquiry on which representatives of opposition parties are often invited to sit. The initiative towards the setting up of these commissions may originate with an opposition group or even an opposition back-bencher. In the field of foreign policy the Advisory Council for Foreign Affairs, composed of members drawn from all the four larger parties—thus excluding the Communists—is expected to be consulted on all questions of major importance before a decision is taken. Institutions apart, the Social Democrats in government have consulted with opposition leaders on a wide variety of topics, ranging from economic problems to the introduction of right-hand traffic (a reform reached by inter-party agreement some time after being overwhelmingly rejected at a consultative popular referendum). More generally, the old ideal of *saklighet*—objectivity, unprejudiced respect for evidence, a spirit of cool rational appraisal—continues to have an effect on the political climate. It influences work on commissions of inquiry, for example, and also on the parliamentary standing committees—specialist bodies composed of members elected on a proportional representation basis and customarily re-elected year after year for as long as they care (and are entitled) to sit. Finally, there is the point that the Government has not claimed a monopoly of public office but has now and again disposed of some vacancy to the opposition, e.g. membership of an administrative board (very occasionally the director-generalship) or the governorship of a province.

All of this tends towards lowering the temperature of political controversy and creating good personal relationships between the members of different parties, but, of course, the power remains very much in the hands of the Government: the power, for example, to select the membership of commissions of inquiry and, of course, to use a parliamentary majority to enforce the Government's will when differences appear. The coin has also an obverse side. In the field of economic policy in particular, the opposition parties—especially the Conservatives and Liberals—have experienced some sense of frustration in the post-war years as a result of the increase in co-operation between Government, on the one hand, and the large organizations on both sides of the labour market on the other. This issue first assumed prominence in connection with the rather surprising subject of civil service pay awards. In these, however, the Riksdag has a traditional interest, so that the opposition was provoked to complain that Parliament was being presented with *faits accomplis* by virtue of the fact that direct negotiations between the two sides had led to agreements binding on both.[22] More recently there have been complaints about "Harpsund democracy"—the practice of holding conferences between government ministers and, first and foremost, representatives of commerce and industry at the prime ministerial country estate at Harpsund in Södermanland. Opposition leaders have been invited to Harpsund on occasion, too, but separately from the industrialists, bankers, insurance men, small businessmen, pensioners, etc. From the Government point of view, all this is simply "consultative democracy" in action, and assurances have been given that no underhand commitments are entered into at these latter conferences.[23] But the exclusion of the opposition, the private character of the discussions, and, it may be added, the favourable comments which have occasionally been made on the usefulness of the proceedings by, for example, the *Swedish Employers' Journal*,[24] have all helped to give rise to disgruntled comments in the opposition Press. Thus there have been complaints that the corporative state has begun to appear;[25] that the Government has been quietly stealing Liberal clothing;[26] that those who go to the conferences will wish for

[22] The question is discussed in G. Heckscher, *Staten och organisationerna*, 2nd rev. edn., Ko-operativa förbundets bokförlag, Stockholm, 1951, pp. 249–51, 255–6.

[23] E.g. by the Prime Minister in a radio discussion with Ohlin on 16 October 1961.

[24] As quoted, for example, in *Östergötlands-Folkblad* (Social Democratic paper), 27 February 1964.

[25] *Expressen* (Liberal), 27 March 1961.

[26] *Göteborgs Handels— och Sjöfartstidning* (Liberal), 27 March 1961.

self-interested reasons to stand well with the Government;[27] that the major decisions are passing into the hands of a technocratic oligarchy;[28] and, *passim*, that power has been passing from the place where it rightfully belongs—the Riksdag. Behind all this can be discerned at times the fear that industry and commerce might be seduced from their traditional allegiance. But it is hard to resist the conclusion that there is a certain element of shadow-boxing about the criticisms just the same, given that politics—in Sweden as elsewhere—are so closely enmeshed with the business of trying to minimize unemployment, increase exports, stimulate productivity, and make full use of national resources. To some extent, as one Social Democratic newspaper put it—making sardonic use of the Swedish variety of the proverb—this is a case of the fox calling the rowan-berries sour.[29]

CURRENTS OF REFORM: CONSTITUTIONAL REFORM AND ITS ORIGINS

The long period of single-party dominance has not led to a hardening of the arteries of government. One sign of this which may appropriately be examined in the present context is the flurry of reforms—actual, on the stocks, and under discussion—which has characterized the last 18 years or so in the field of Swedish political institutions. It cannot be said that these reforms have, as a general rule, owed much to popular clamour or to social discontent. The public has on the whole been indifferent about them: they are primarily the result of the activity of the politicians and administrators who work the system. Consequently, although over much of the field they have provoked considerable debate, that debate has been mainly carried on in the Press (which is overwhelmingly party-orientated in Sweden) and within the parties and the Riksdag. At general elections the more bread-and-butter issues of politics have predominated. Even within the parties, indeed, there is some evidence that, in the earlier stages, at least, the leadership has been more

[27] *Kvällsposten* (Conservative), 29 March 1961.
[28] *Eskilstuna Kuriren* (Liberal), 7 and 8 November 1963.
[29] *Norrländska Social-Demokraten*, 29 March 1961.

heavily engaged than the rank and file: only 3 out of 173 motions at a Social Democratic Party congress in 1964 dealt with constitutional reform questions, for example, although these questions had been receiving considerable Press coverage for some time.

The issue of constitutional reform arose in the early 1950's—not, it may be noted, out of constitutional crisis but rather from a desire to modernize and rationalize the basic laws. These latter were markedly antiquated in some respects, and the idea of an overhaul commanded general acceptance. It was not just a case of a lawyer's tidying-up operation, so to speak: written prescription was felt to be having a clogging effect on the machinery of government at certain points. From this it was felt to be a natural step to carry the process of rational scrutiny a stage further and to subject virtually the entire constitutional framework to a critical review.[30] Party political considerations inevitably began to make themselves apparent as soon as major substantive reform came under discussion. The result has been a positive rash of reform proposals but rather slow progress in the matter of practical results. A general overhaul of the Constitution has not yet been achieved, but a considerable partial reform has just now been enacted.

The Swedish Constitution is unusual in consisting of four separate documents. The earliest of these, the Instrument of Government (*Regeringsformen*), dates from 1809 and is not unfairly regarded as the oldest written constitution still in force in Europe because it provides the framework into which the others have fitted. The second document, the Act of Succession (*Successionsordningen*), was passed one year after the Instrument of Government and, as the name indicates, regulates the succession to the throne. The third, the Riksdag Act (*Riksdagsordningen*), marks the emergence in 1866 of the present bicameral legislature. Finally, there is the Freedom of the Press Act (*Tryckfrihetsförordningen*). This only dates from 1969, when it replaced an earlier model, and has in consequence not been affected by the agitation for constitutional reform.

[30] Especially since Parliament had approved motions asking for inquiry into particular parts of the system, e.g. the electoral laws, in the immediately preceding years.

Constitutional amendment is not a difficult process in Sweden[31] and many amendments have in fact been made. In the case of the Instrument of Government in particular these have been so numerous as to create a patchwork of clauses from many different dates. The predominant spirit of this document, however, has, until the current overhaul, been that of 1809, so it is hardly surprising that there should have been a wide gap until now between legal text and political reality. To quote from the terms of reference of the four-party Commission on the Constitution which was set up in 1954:

> One should not be blind to the fact that our Constitution—even in parts where the letter of the law still has undoubted normative force—builds to a large extent on concepts and ideas that were current at the time of the appearance of the Constitution close on a century and a half ago but that have lost most of their significance in our day. One pervasive characteristic, for example, is the conception of a dualism, a state of opposition between government and popular assembly—a conception which has as its background circumstances at the time of the appearance of the Constitution but which has lost its basis in reality with our present-day parliamentary democracy. The age of our Constitution is also betrayed by the fact that it only mirrors very imperfectly the values and goals of our own time.[32]

It may be mentioned here in passing that the dualism referred to in the above passage still colours the working of the Swedish political system. It is not surprising that the settlement of 1809 should have embodied an attempt to check and balance the powers of both King and Parliament. Most of the previous century had been marked by the abuse of power by each side successively. But clearly a dualism between executive and legislature is incompatible with a modern cabinet government system, and in fact the surviving traces of the old regime are chiefly interesting as constitutional curiosities. Ministers, for example, are still excluded from appearing before most of the standing committees of the Riksdag. But, of course, party loyalty ensures that government Bills will pass in substantially the same form as that in which they left their departments, at least whenever the Government has a majority. It would scarcely be

[31] See below, pp. 28 and 131.

[32] SOU, 1963: 17, p. 8.

unfair to say, therefore, that the chief effect of the exclusion rule is to strengthen the tradition that government Bills should include lengthy written preambles and declarations of ministerial intent. The future of this particular survival seems precarious.[33] Again, the minutes of the formal meetings of the Government are handed over annually for scrutiny to one of the parliamentary standing committees.[34] It is hardly to be imagined that differences within the Government at the formative stage of policy making are thereby brought to the notice of an expectant opposition. The minutes serve chiefly as a record of business decided, and the procedure is mainly useful as a peg on which to hang reviews of administrative practice. The celebrated office of Ombudsman, incidentally, began life in 1809 more as a parliamentary check to improper governmental influence on individual civil servants than as the guarantor of citizens' rights which it has subsequently become.

The terms of reference of the 1954 Commission on the Constitution, as was said above, went beyond the relatively simple task of tidying up legal texts—in fact they included an injunction to undertake "a comprehensive review of the working problems of democracy" and listed a series of particular topics for review. The programme was a lengthy one and it is not surprising that the Commission laboured at it for a long time. A series of study documents came out on specific aspects of the subject-matter, but 9 years were to elapse before the appearance of the final reports.

The immediate results of these labours were rather meagre in terms of constitutional amendments passed. Thus one of the topics assigned to the Commission for review had been the role of the major interest groups in the political system. The main report, predictably, contained only a few generalities on this theme: this was considered to be hardly an area for much formal regulation.[35]

[33] See below, pp. 60–62, for a further discussion of the exclusion rule.

[34] See Chapter 5, pp.123 ff.

[35] In addition, an extensive review of the current position had already been published under the auspices of the Commission—SOU, 1961:21, Lars Foyer, *Former för kontakt och samverkan mellan staten och organisationerna.*

The Commission did, however, do something to meet the complaint that the Riksdag had been bypassed by direct negotiations between the Government and the relevant unions in the matter of civil service salaries. It successfully recommended the setting up of a parliamentary "pay delegation", composed on the usual proportional representation principle, to represent the Riksdag at the negotiating stage of the discussions and to act on behalf of the Riksdag at the decision-making stage. Secondly, and in accordance with another recommendation, the rules governing civil service terms of appointment have been made more flexible by being taken out of the Constitution for insertion into ordinary statute law. Thirdly, the age of accession to the throne has been raised from 21 to 25. This last change is examined further in the next chapter,[36] but it may be observed meantime that the Commission report sparked off a brisk controversy about whether or not Sweden should continue to be a constitutional monarchy and helped to revive a latent current of republicanism in both the Social Democratic and Liberal parties—all this despite the fact that the form of the State was not included in the Commission's terms of reference. The Commission had, however, been charged with the task of committing to paper the rules of the parliamentary game; this involved it in an analysis of the function of the head of State in a regime in which "all political power comes from the Swedish people";[37] the nature of the exercise and the recommendations made by the Commission inevitably gave rise to a wider debate.

Apart from these and a few other scattered small-scale reforms—of which possibly the most significant was the lowering of the voting age to 20 in 1966[38]—the Commission's proceedings can be said to have paved the way for one major change and to have initiated a process of slow fermentation which has not yet fully worked itself out.

[36] See below, p. 38.

[37] *Proposed Instrument of Government*, chap. 1, section 1.

[38] Those who have reached the age of 19 in the calendar year before election year are now entitled to vote under the terms of the 1968/9 constitutional amendments.

The Cameral Reform

The major reform impending is the abolition of the Upper House of the Swedish Riksdag and the creation of a single chamber somewhat larger than the present Lower House. The Upper House, it should be said at this stage, is a chamber of 151 members indirectly elected for an 8-year term by provincial and major city councils; the Lower House has 233 members and is directly elected for a 4-year term. The Commission split on the question of abolishing the Upper House, but a large majority favoured a unicameral system.[39] The details of the proposed change, however, aroused so much dissension between the parties that no immediate headway could be made. The Social Democrats, briefly, wished to preserve some sort of a link between local and parliamentary elections, while the opposition parties set themselves against this. The situation had its ironies. The differences between the two houses have been narrowing steadily since the turn of the century, and the theoretical arguments in favour of a second chamber have become harder to maintain with the advance of radical democratic thought. Yet the fact that the Upper House reflects the public opinion of anything up to 11 years back (because of its indirect election by the larger local government authorities and its 8-year term of office) meant that it came under heavy periodic attack from the opposition parties for cushioning the Social Democrats from the full effects of adverse currents of opinion in the country. This situation recurred as recently as 1966, when the Social Democrats gained a seat in the Upper House and thus recovered their overall majority in joint cameral votes at the very time when they were suffering their heavy reverse in the local government elections.

In March 1967 the four major parties at length reached agreement in principle on the question of parliamentary reform—as a result of the activities of a four-party preparatory committee set up under the chairmanship of a Social Democratic Provincial Governor, Valter Åman, in order to find out how much could be achieved quickly in

[39] An alternative (dissenting) report was submitted by two members—Herr Wahlund (Centre) and Herr Ahlkvist (Social Democrat).

the way of a partial reform as a stage towards the complete overhaul of the Constitution. It was decided that the Upper House should be swept away and that a unicameral legislature should be created having 350 seats: 310 of these seats are scheduled to be distributed between territorial constituencies on the usual pattern except that the allocation will be based on the number of electors and not, as now, on the total population figure. The remaining 40 seats are to be distributed between the parties on a national basis and according to the proportional representation principle. There will, however, be a requirement that a party must have 4 per cent of the national vote before it can qualify for a share of the national pool and 12 per cent of the vote in a constituency before it can qualify for a seat there. The new legislature is intended to have a 3-year term as compared with 4 years for the Lower House at present, and the elections are to be held on the same day as elections to local government authorities throughout the country (these latter elections are currently held at 4-year intervals halfway between general elections to the Lower House).

These reforms were incorporated into constitutional amendments and given their first approval by Parliament before the 1968 general elections. They have now been passed into law by the new Riksdag in accordance with the usual amendment procedure—initiation by one Riksdag, final decision by the next after the electorate has had the opportunity to make its feelings known. The present Riksdag will thus itself be dissolved in September 1970 and elections will then be held under the new dispensation. The details of the scheme vary somewhat from those proposed by unicameralists on the original Commission on the Constitution. The alteration of the parliamentary term and the provision that national elections shall occur on the same day as local are both new and have come about largely as a result of Social Democratic pressure. The provision for national seats, another innovation, follows Danish and Icelandic practice rather than the Commission line. The fact remains that it was the Commission which provided the initial impetus.

Other Reforms

The party leaders also agreed in the Spring of 1967 to a number of other changes whose origins can likewise be traced to the Commission report. As part of the process of writing the rules of modern parliamentary government into the constitution, for example, it is proposed that the King shall be required to consult the Speaker and the party leaders before choosing a Prime Minister. This simply follows existing practice. Again—also in accordance with a Commission recommendation—votes of no confidence are to be introduced into parliamentary procedure. They may be tabled either against the Government collectively or against an individual minister by one-tenth of the total membership of the new chamber (the Commission would have allowed any one MP to set the machinery in motion). They will then need an absolute majority of those voting to pass. The chief significance of this new parliamentary weapon, so far as can be judged at the time of writing, would seem to be symbolic: the Riksdag is given, for the first time, a formal means of ejecting a government or a minister forfeiting its confidence.[40]

The impact of the Commission is not hard to trace in these developments. It may also be seen in some of the recent reforms that have been carried out in the executive sector. The decentralized nature of the Swedish administrative structure—a basic feature of the Swedish governmental system which will be more closely examined later[41]—has made it easier for the Government and the departments of State to concentrate on the task of setting policy norms while leaving the administrative agencies to get on with the more routine work. Nevertheless, the constantly expanding scope of the planning function has necessitated organizational changes at governmental, departmental, and board levels alike. New ancillary agencies have been attached to the Cabinet to help it in this field, and

[40] The change may also be viewed as the modern equivalent to the rules governing the answerability of ministers in §107 of the Instrument of Government—rules which for a long time have failed to serve their original purpose. (See Chapter 7, pp. 158–9.)

[41] See below, Chapter 3.

to some extent they follow lines suggested in the Commission report.[42] The structure of the departments of State was recast in 1965 with the aim of strengthening the planning function—here much of the spadework was done by an inquiry carried out by one of the Ministers without Portfolio[43] who provide a useful *masse de manœuvre* within the Swedish Cabinet system. Again, despite administrative decentralization, the Government and the departments still have to deal with certain categories of small-scale administrative business. The process has therefore begun of devolving as many as possible of these comparatively unimportant questions to the decentralized sector of the administration. This, too, was a subject to which the Commission had devoted attention and on which it had some useful practical proposals to make. But the more far-reaching suggestion made by the Commission for a large expansion in the area of ministerial responsibility as part of the process of removing less important matters from the Cabinet agenda was not well received and has been shelved.[44]

These matters will come up again in what follows. Meanwhile the current large instalment of constitutional reform, as was mentioned above, is designed to be the first major step on the road to a complete overhaul of the basic laws. The inter-party preparatory group is therefore continuing its work and is expected to be busy for a number of years yet.

[42] See below, pp. 55–57.
[43] On Ministers without Portfolio, see pp. 42–45.
[44] See pp. 51–52.

CHAPTER 2

King and Council

THE ROLE OF THE MONARCHY

The Swedish Constitution of 1809 formally vested the executive power in the monarch:

> The King alone shall govern the realm . . . he shall, however, . . . seek the information and advice of a Council of State, to which [he] shall call and appoint capable, experienced, honourable and generally respected native Swedish subjects.[1]

Similarly:

> If the King wishes to declare war or to conclude peace, he shall convene all the members of the Council of State in extraordinary Council, lay before them the causes and circumstances to be considered, and ask for their opinion concerning the matter . . . the King may then make and execute such decision as he considers in the best interest of the realm.[2]

Again, "the King was to be Commander-in-Chief of the armed forces",[3] and in this capacity he was exempt from the general rule that the Council of State should be consulted, being obliged to confer only with the Minister of Defence.[4] He could not be held personally responsible for any of the decisions which he took.[5]

The Instrument of Government of 1809, from which these rules are drawn, was not, however, designed to act as a blueprint for royal absolutism. Sweden had just experienced a period of royal absolutism, and it had ended in military defeat by Russia, the loss of

[1] *Regeringsform*, article 4, before the 1968/9 revisions. The citations of the other articles of the Instrument of Government in this section also refer to the unrevised version.

[2] *Ibid.*, article 13. [3] *Ibid.*, article 14. [4] *Ibid.*, article 15.

[5] *Ibid.*, article 3.

Finland, and the abdication and flight of the King (Gustav IV). An earlier period of parliamentary rule, during which the monarchy had been reduced to a cipher—the so-called Era of Liberty (1719–72)—had proved almost equally disastrous. The constitution makers of 1809 were thus resolved to strike a balance between the two extremes. They gave the King an active share in the making of public policy, but they made his powers subject to safeguards and confined them within carefully staked out limits.

The chief safeguards were contained in the rules relating to ministerial responsibility. A selection of these rules may be given to indicate their general character. The ministers (councillors) were to meet together with the King in Council, and the Constitution prescribed that virtually all matters of government should be submitted to the King in Council and be decided there.[6] Such members of the Council of State as were present, "being held responsible for their advice", were "positively obliged to express and explain their opinions", which were to be entered in the minutes.[7] They were then liable to impeachment if the Riksdag (the Swedish Parliament) discovered from the minutes that they had given unconstitutional advice or abetted the King in any way in unconstitutional action.[8] They were further liable to have the Riksdag petition the King for their removal from office if it discovered from the minutes that they had not "paid due regard to the welfare of the state"[9] or that they had failed to perform their duties "with impartiality, zeal, ability and energy".[9] The King, who appointed them, might have been reluctant to dismiss them; but in the last resort it was the Riksdag which had the edge, for it alone had the power to levy taxation[10] and to determine the ends on which public moneys should be spent.[11]

These rules, which formed part of a system based upon the principle of the separation of powers modified to suit Swedish circumstances, have an archaic ring today. They have been made largely obsolete by the arrival of modern parliamentary government, which

[6] *Regeringsform*, article 7. There was one exception to this rule, already noted in the text—certain military questions.

[7] *Ibid.*, article 9. [8] *Ibid.*, article 106. [9] *Ibid.*, article 107.

[10] *Ibid.*, article 57. [11] *Ibid.*, article 62.

has had the usual effect of transferring power decisively from monarch to ministers, and they have now been largely deleted by the 1968/9 partial constitutional reform. Thus the rules concerning ministerial responsibility for advice, the monarch's powers over peace and war, and the handling of military questions have been rescinded. Government business is still, however, finally disposed of in the presence of the King in Council (*Konselj*). These formal Council of State meetings, which usually take place on Fridays at the Royal Palace in Stockholm, are traditionally primarily a rubber-stamping and recording device: the real decisions are taken earlier in Cabinet (*Statsrådsberedning*).[12] The evidence is that important matters are sometimes raised informally with the King before the council meeting. This is done chiefly for information purposes, but it gives the King a chance to offer his advice and even, on rare occasions, to influence the course of events.[13]

Another characteristically Swedish device which provides the King with an opportunity to enjoy the classical rights of a constitutional monarch to be consulted, to encourage, and to warn, is the Advisory Council for Foreign Affairs (*Utrikesnämnden*). The Advisory Council was created in 1921 as a successor to an earlier "Secret Committee" which the King could summon at will to consult and inform about important questions of foreign policy. The Council is a small body representative of the major parties in Parliament (not, therefore, including the Communists). It "should" be consulted "before all matters of major importance relating to foreign affairs are decided",[14] and it is to be given all the relevant information. "The King convenes the Council as often as business demands, and is chairman of the Council when he is present. In the King's absence, the Prime Minister, or in the latter's absence, the Minister for Foreign Affairs, takes the chair."[15] The evidence is that the

[12] See below, p. 53 f.

[13] Nils Andrén, *Modern Swedish Government*, Almkvist & Wiksell, Stockholm, 1961, p. 106; G. Heckscher, *Svensk statsförvaltning i arbete*, 2nd edn., Norstedt, Stockholm, 1958, p. 215; Allan Ingelson, *Officiellt*, Bokförlaget natur och kultur, Stockholm, 1947, pp. 49–50; Allan Nordenstam, Hur regeringen arbetar, *Statsvetenskaplig Tidskrift*, 1957, pp. 245–56.

[14] RF, article 54.

[15] Riksdag Act (*Riksdagsordning*), article 49.

Council is usually convened when important issues of foreign policy arise and that the King usually presides at such meetings.[16] The then Privy Secretary to the Ministry of Foreign Affairs has recorded, for example, that "it seemed natural . . . to hear the Advisory Council" when the Germans requested permission for the passage of a division through Sweden to Finland in midsummer 1941.[17] King Gustav V certainly seems to have given strong support to his Prime Minister, at least immediately after the Council meeting, in agreeing to the request—though not, as was for a time supposed, to the extent of threatening abdication if the request were rejected.[18]

Parliamentary government is generally reckoned to have won final acceptance in Sweden in 1917. Active and open interventions by the King in political affairs thus persisted into the earlier years of this century: probably the most dramatic instance occurred in February 1914 when Gustav V forced the resignation of Karl Staaff's Liberal Government over defence policy.[19] The Liberal–Social Democratic coalition government of 1917–20 under Nils Edén was, however, too firmly based in popular support to be gainsaid, and the democratization of the franchise which it carried out ensured that the King's loss of power would be final. Gustav V was energetic from time to time thereafter in proferring advice, notably in the matter of ministerial appointments, and he was assisted in this by the fact that the period from 1920 to 1932 was one of unstable minority government. But he could never do more than advise, and he met with diminishing success.[20]

Since 1917, then, the monarchy in Sweden has evolved into a modern constitutional monarchy bound by the rules of the parliamentary game. The gap between its formal and its real powers has widened in consequence. The elimination of this gap was entrusted

[16] For a general account of the Advisory Council and its work, see N. C. M. Elder, Parliament and foreign policy in Sweden, *Political Studies*, 1953, pp. 193–206. See also below, pp. 169–71.

[17] Erik Boheman, *På Vakt*, Norstedt, Stockholm, 1964, p. 167.

[18] *Ibid.*, pp. 167–9.

[19] See D. V. Verney, *Parliamentary Reform in Sweden*, Oxford, 1957, pp. 185–91.

[20] See Dankwart A. Rustow, *op. cit.*, p. 216.

in 1954 by Erlander's Social Democrat–Farmers' Party coalition government to the Commission on the Constitution as part of the wider operation of modernizing and revising the basic laws as a whole. The Commission represented all the major parties: of its original 8 members, 4 were Social Democrats, 2 Liberals (or People's Party—one of these was the party secretary), 1 an Agrarian, and 1 a Conservative. The terms of reference of the Commission excluded any change in the monarchical character of the State, so that the inquiry came to the conclusion that its chief task so far as the monarchy was concerned was to produce "a codification and clarification of the present order".[21] The results were embodied in a complete draft constitution published in 1963 with accompanying commentary.[22] The main points raised in connection with the monarchy are worth a brief review.

The Commission began by asking itself what should be the duties of a head of State in a modern parliamentary democracy. Whether or not the head of State is a king or a president was taken to be irrelevant in this context, since the duties remain the same in either case. "If a country is very large, or if diverse peoples are combined in the one State, or if sharp cleavages divide the people—these are some of the circumstances which may be cited to justify the grant of special duties to the head of state as a political leader or as an arbiter between contending factions."[23] None of these conditions are fulfilled in Sweden, so the duties of the head of State should be confined to the minimum necessary for the smooth working of the parliamentary regime. They are in fact so confined at present.

"The chief task proper to the head of state in a parliamentary democracy", says the report, "is to assist in the formation of governments, in the first instance by selecting the Prime Minister."[24] Detailed rules to cover all contingencies (and thus to reduce the discretionary power of the head of State to zero) are impracticable. The determining factor must, however, always be the party position in the Riksdag, and so the Commission proposed to write into the new

[21] SOU, 1963: 17, p. 138.

[22] *Ibid.*: 16 for the draft constitution; 17 for the commentary.

[23] *Ibid.*: 17, p. 137. [24] *Ibid.*, p. 138.

Instrument of Government the requirement that the King shall consult the Speaker and the representatives of party groups in the Riksdag before appointing the Prime Minister.[25] This rule was based on the existing procedure in unclear parliamentary situations. In 1957, for example, the King consulted the Speakers of both houses and party leaders when the Farmers' Party resigned from their coalition with the Social Democrats. On that occasion the three non-Socialist opposition parties had a majority in the Riksdag, and the King investigated the possibility of their forming a coalition. In the event the project failed, and the Social Democrats formed a minority government instead. It may perhaps be added that the Commission suggested no special rule for filling a vacancy in the premiership caused by the death or retirement through ill health, etc., of the incumbent. In such a situation, however, there is a precedent ready to hand: in 1946 the King waited until the Social Democrats had elected Erlander their leader before filling the vacancy caused by the death of Per-Albin Hansson.

Ministers other than the Prime Minister, according to the Commission draft, should be appointed by the King on the Prime Minister's recommendation. The expectation plainly is that, in line with recent practice, the King would automatically accept the Prime Minister's recommendation. Again, the right to dismiss ministers would be given to the King: the suggested rules are so clearly derived from the principle of parliamentary government as to need no special comment. The right to dissolve the Riksdag would belong to the King but could only be used on the initiative of the Prime Minister. The Commission recognized the possibility that the King might refuse to agree to a request for a dissolution. "It does not automatically follow", they said, "that the desire of the Government to put itself to the proof with the electorate should be given precedence over the views of a Riksdag majority."[26] In order to be justified in refusing a dissolution, therefore, the King must first make

[25] The Commission report, it will be noted, lays down that "the Speaker" shall be consulted. This is because it proposes the creation of a unicameral legislature.

[26] SOU, 1963: 17, p. 141.

sure that an alternative government can be formed with majority support. In the normal case, of course, the King would agree to the Prime Minister's wishes—as happened in 1958 when the minority Social Democratic Government asked for and got the first dissolution on political grounds for over 40 years after being defeated in the Riksdag. The proposal to give formal status to the King's power to refuse a dissolution has been criticized on the grounds that no head of State should have discretion in the matter because of the risks of political involvement. At the end of the day this criticism has triumphed, so that on this particular point the Commission report has been overtaken by events: the 1968/9 constitutional amendments provide that a dissolution shall be granted at the request of the Prime Minister.

The Commission recommended that the King should continue to lead the discussions in the Advisory Council for Foreign Affairs "when he is present".[27] It wished, however, to cut down drastically the amount of government business required to go through the formal Council of State.[28] It wished also to restrict the King to the simple acceptance or rejection in Council meetings of proposals already made by the Cabinet.[29] This virtually recognized the rubber-stamp character of these Council proceedings, since the rejection of a proposal by the King would obviously be either the cause or the effect of a constitutional crisis of the first magnitude. The changes suggested would be likely to reduce the range of information available to the King, but not to any significant extent: the more important questions would continue to come to King in Council, and the Commission made it clear that there would be no bar to the King being notified of them, and of his government's views, in advance of the Council meeting. Whether or not the King would be deprived of any opportunity effectively to advise and warn ministers on the basis of the information he receives is obscure, though certainly the rules seem to discourage any royal influence.

[27] *Draft for a new Instrument of Government*, chapter 4, article 7.

[28] For details, see below, p. 50.

[29] The commission would have formal minutes kept at Cabinet meetings for subsequent parliamentary scrutiny.

Another recommendation of the Commission report, and one that has been accepted and passed by Erlander's Social Democratic Government,[30] is that the age of accession to the throne should be raised from 21 to 25. This is the second time within 20 years that the accession age has been raised: before 1949 it used to be 18. Two main arguments were urged by the Commission in support of the change: that the dignified nature of the office required it, and that it would allow an opportunity to the heir apparent for a more prolonged period of "academic and other studies".[31] Should the throne became vacant when the next in line is not of age to succeed, the gist of the rather complicated rules at present in force is that "the Riksdag shall have the power . . . to appoint one, three or five regents to exercise the government in the King's name . . . until he attains his majority".[32] Since the present monarch, King Gustav VI, is 88 years of age, and the Crown Prince, Carl Gustav, is 23, the recent change in the law means that the latter could not succeed to the throne in the event of a vacancy until 1971 and that the regency rule just referred to would take effect in the meantime.

The present Constitution contains a whole set of clauses providing for the conduct of affairs of State when the King is absent through sickness or foreign travel or—more picturesquely—when he "goes on a military expedition or visits distant parts of the realm".[33] Briefly, the Commission wanted to modernize these rules. Thus, for example, it recommended that a regency in the event of sickness or foreign travel should continue to be exercised by the Crown Prince or, failing him, by other princes in line of succession, provided that the Prince in question has reached the age of 25 and is not himself incapacitated by sickness, absence abroad, etc. But if no Prince should be available, the Commission proposed that "for practical reasons" the regency should be exercised by the Speaker of the Riksdag and not, as now, by the entire Council of State.[34]

The line of succession to the Swedish throne is regulated by the

[30] Proposition 1964: 140 passed in 1965.
[31] SOU, 1963: 17, p. 219.
[32] RF, article 93.
[33] *Ibid.*, article 43.
[34] SOU, 1963: 17, p. 135.

Act of Succession of 1810, one of the four constitutional laws.[35] Succession is restricted to male heirs. The Act contains a clause—reflecting a clause in the Instrument of Government—that in the event of the male line dying out, the Riksdag shall elect a new royal house.[36] This the Commission wished to modify in order to leave the Riksdag free in such a case to elect a President if it so desires. Otherwise they would leave the Act unchanged, in accordance with their terms of reference. It may be added that three members of the Commission—one Liberal, one Agrarian, and a Social Democrat—urged in a minority report that women should be eligible to succeed to the throne. Two of the same three members—the Agrarian and the Social Democrat—also wished the age of accession to remain unchanged. The Conservatives have also expressed strong support for the introduction of female succession but were deprived of a signature on the final report by the death of their representative on the Commission.

Progress on the Commission report, as was mentioned in the Introduction, has in general been rather slow and deliberate, and the final outcome in some sectors is still uncertain. This applies in particular to the recommendations concerning the monarchy. These recommendations have nevertheless been discussed at some length for three reasons. Firstly, they attempted a "codification and clarification" of the rules then in force. Secondly, they helped to pave the way for the recent revision of the rules. Thirdly, they have given rise to a controversy which has expanded markedly beyond the original terms of reference. Some commentators have argued, for example, that the true logic of parliamentary government requires that the King shall in no circumstances be able to pursue a policy counter to the government of the day. From this point of view the Commission's draft gave him unwarrantable liberty. "Taken as a whole", to cite an extreme statement, "these royal powers mean that parliamentarism as generally understood would not survive if the draft goes

[35] The others being the Instrument of Government (RF), the Riksdag Act (*Riksdagsordningen*, RO), and the Freedom of the Press Act (*Tryckfrihetsförordningen*, TFO).

[36] Act of Succession, article 9.

through."[37] Others fear that the position of the monarchy has been undermined.[38] The first clause of all in the proposed Constitution reads: "All state power in the Swedish realm comes from the Swedish people"[39]—and the terms of the Commission report make clear that the duties of a head of State in a parliamentary democracy are fully interchangeable between monarch and president.[40]

Certainly the report has helped to awaken quite a strong current of republicanism in the Social Democratic Party, especially among the younger generation.[41] At inter-party discussions held in November 1965 in Saltsjöbaden under the chairmanship of Olof Palme, then a Social Democratic minister, it was agreed that a complete overhaul of the Constitution would not be practicable before 1972 or 1973, but that a partial reform should be attempted in 1968 or 1969. In the course of these November talks the Social Democrats made it clear that they wished to put an examination of the powers of the head of State high on the agenda for any partial constitutional reform. Then, in January 1966, came a Riksdag motion signed by thirty-three Social Democrats calling for the setting up of a special inquiry to investigate the position of the head of State in a parliamentary democracy —including the position of a democratically elected head of State in a republic. The sponsors made it clear that they intended no reflection on the reigning monarch, nor did they envisage any change taking place in his lifetime. The reference to a republic was deleted in committee, and the motion in this modified form was passed in the Upper House by 72 votes to 61 and in the Lower by 108 votes to 98. It received the support of the Social Democratic Prime Minister, Erlander, and of the leaders of that party, and all the Social Democrats voted for it—along with the handful of Communists. The Conservatives and Centre (Farmers') Party voted against, along

[37] H. Tingsten, *Skall kungamakten stärkas?*, Bonniers, Stockholm, 1964, p. 31.

[38] E.g. N. Herlitz, *1969 års regeringsform?*, Norstedts, Stockholm, 1963, pp. 30–44.

[39] Draft RF, chapter 1, article 1.

[40] SOU, 1963: 17, p. 137.

[41] A pamphlet written by L. Andersson, I. Carlsson, and A. Gustafsson (*Författningsreform—nytt alternativ*, Tidens förlag, Stockholm, 1963) may be taken as typical of the trend.

with most of the Liberals. In the course of the debate Palme made it plain that a discussion of the position of the head of State would involve a discussion of the type of regime into which he should fit.

In the event the partial constitutional reform has been agreed and is being put into effect while the question of the position of the head of State has been referred for consideration to the inter-party committee which is working on the task of completing the overhaul of the Constitution. A decision on the future form of State has thus been deferred and the issue is still an open one. Looking back on the whole episode, one is reminded of Bagehot's remark: "When there is a select committee on the Queen, the charm of royalty will be gone."[42]

THE COUNCIL OF STATE: COMPOSITION

There is no Cabinet in Sweden in the sense of a clearly differentiated inner ring of ministers at the directive centre of a larger government. All members of the Council of State have an equal right to attend the Cabinet meetings which precede the formal meetings of the King in Council. Cabinet meetings in the Swedish context are thus meetings of the entire Government in the absence of the King and, as mentioned earlier, it is here that the real decisions are taken. The Prime Minister and the Minister for Foreign Affairs enjoy precedence over the rest of the Government, as one might expect. The other ministers, whether or not they head departments, officially have co-equal rank. However, a certain *ex officio* pre-eminence has tended to attach in practice to the Finance Minister, and the vagaries of politics, or the force of personality, have naturally resulted at times in the *de facto* rise of one or two other ministers. Sometimes, too, some Ministers without Portfolio have seemed in the nature of the case to occupy an auxiliary position.

Every department has a minister in charge, and the number of departments is now fixed by legislation passed through the Riksdag in the ordinary way (up to 1941 a constitutional amendment had been required). Twelve departments are now provided for: Justice,

[42] Walter Bagehot, *The English Constitution*, Oxford University Press, 1949, p. 53.

Foreign Affairs, Defence, Social Welfare, Communications, Finance, Education (until 1968, Church Affairs and Education), Agriculture, Commerce, Interior, Civil Service Affairs and, newly, Industrial Affairs. It is, of course, the small number of the departments which makes it possible for every minister to have a seat in Cabinet (and the small number of departments is itself to be explained partly as a byproduct of the decentralized administrative system).

The Prime Minister may choose to head a department, as, for example, Axel Pehrsson did in 1936, when he took over the Ministry of Agriculture in the short-lived Farmers' Party Government of that summer. But this is exceptional. It is much more usual for the Prime Minister to count as one of the Ministers without Portfolio (*konsultativa statsråd*). The Constitution lays down that there shall be at least three of these, and that "at least two must have held civil office".[43] This means state office other than in the established (Lutheran) Church or in the armed services. Further details are left to be settled by ordinary legislation, and currently, under a 1967 Act, a maximum of seven Ministers without Portfolio is prescribed. The past two decades have seen a steady increase in the number of Ministers without Portfolio, and governments have grown in consequence to about the size of the smaller British peacetime cabinets. (The present one has a total membership of eighteen.)

The device of Ministers without Portfolio has some interesting features in Swedish practice. The requirement that at least two of them shall have held civil office was originally designed to ensure that the Council of State had the services of ministers with a high degree of legal and administrative expertize to assist it to discharge the duty of acting as a court of final appeal in the hearing of administrative appeals (*besvär*). This function of government has now become less important, however,[44] and the ministers who are appointed because of these special skills have been adapted to other uses. They divide up the departments between them by agreement, so that each acts as legal adviser on request to a set group of departments;

[43] RF, article 6.

[44] Especially since the creation of a Supreme Administrative Court in 1909 (see Chapter 6).

they scrutinize the texts of government Bills and draft orders, checking in the process the compatibility of proposed with existing law; and they survey the terms of reference of the numerous commissions of inquiry (*kommittéer*), which bulk so large in the Swedish political system, in order to avoid duplication and standardize practice.[45] They may also be asked, like the other Ministers without Portfolio, to diversify their usual activities on occasion by carrying out special assignments on behalf of the Government as a whole. Thus Rune Hermansson, a judge of appeal and one of the legal experts in the Erlander Government until December 1966, was given the task in June 1963 of undertaking an investigation into the organization and procedures of all government departments except Foreign Affairs—at first sight an improbable assignment, but Swedish departments are very small.

Swedish ministers do not have to be Members of Parliament. In all normal circumstances most of them are, of course—the 1920 de Geer von Sydow Ministry, which was composed *entirely* of civil servants, was a temporary throwback to an earlier age. Usually the exceptions to the rule are to be found in the ranks of the Ministers without Portfolio. Rune Hermansson, for example, who was mentioned above, was a non-party minister without a seat in Parliament. Sven-Eric Nilsson, one of the legal experts in the current government, is a civil servant who had previously been at the head of the Legal Affairs Division in the Ministry of Finance. He exemplifies a different gradation in the scale of political involvement: a non-parliamentarian but a member of the Social Democratic Party. Camilla Odhnoff, another present-day Minister without Portfolio, was brought into the Government in December 1966 without a seat in the Riksdag to specialize in family and youth questions: she had earlier been active in the Social Democratic Women's Organization in Skåne, Sweden's southernmost province, and was also a lecturer in plant physiology at the University of Lund.

[45] H. Meijer, *Kommittépolitik och kommittéarbete*, Gleerup, Lund, 1956, pp. 217 and 222. Also Heckscher, *op. cit.*, p. 214 and Nordenstam, *op. cit.*, *passim.* Nordenstam was himself a Minister without Portfolio, and gives a first-hand account.

Another position in the scale of political involvement among Ministers without Portfolio can be detected in the case of Krister Wickman, who was virtually a second Finance Minister with special responsibilities in the field of trade and economic policy before becoming Minister for Industrial Affairs and who has enjoyed a rapid rise to political eminence. For eight years he occupied a key position within the civil service as Under-Secretary to the Ministry of Finance[46] (after earlier service as the secretary to the Parliamentary Standing Committee on Banking); then (in 1966) he stood successfully for the Upper House in the Social Democratic interest, and a few months later received his ministerial appointment. Then, again, there are the politicians of longer standing like Lennart Geijer, a specialist on rent and labour law and legal adviser to the country's chief union of white-collar workers, who has sat in the Upper House for some years now. The device of Ministers without Portfolio, in short, enables the Swedish Prime Minister both to expand the field of recruitment to cabinet office beyond the parliamentary sphere and to groom able new men for higher office.

When Ministers without Portfolio are used (as they often are) to relieve hard-pressed departmental ministers of particular blocks of work, they take over responsibility for the work in question and operate with the assistance of the relevant departmental staffs. Thus Svante Lundkvist was put in charge of local and provincial government affairs to relieve the Department of the Interior (before, as it happened, later becoming Minister of Communications in charge, *inter alia*, of local and provincial government affairs). It is even possible for a Minister without Portfolio to combine the responsibility for business from different departments. Ulla Lindström, for instance, was Dr. Odhnoff's predecessor in the matter of family and youth questions and had at the same time responsibilities in connection with aid to underdeveloped countries. Finally, Ministers without Portfolio are additionally useful in a bicameral system for

[46] Under-secretaryships are, however, a peculiar type of post, sometimes more accurately regarded as political than as civil service appointments. See below, pp. 83–86.

introducing government business in the other House from that in which the relevant departmental minister is to be found.

Collective Responsibility and the General Absence of Ministerial Responsibility

Swedish ministries observe in practice the principle of collective responsibility and maintain a united front in the face of the world outside. A minister in disagreement with government policy is expected to keep quiet or to resign. Disharmonies of this type are rare, and there have only been two instances of resignations over policy differences in the last 30 years: Rickard Sandler, as Foreign Minister, over the Åland Isles issue in 1939, and Ulla Lindström, as Minister without Portfolio, over the question of the scale of government aid to underdeveloped lands in December 1966.

The position in respect of ministerial responsibility in the narrower sense is more complicated and deserves a closer look. The first point to make clear is perhaps that ministerial responsibility, in the sense of the responsibility of ministers for the conduct of administration within the whole of the area of public policy designated by their departmental titles, does not exist in Sweden. Only in one or two specialized fields, in fact, do Swedish ministers have any formal and direct responsibility for administration. Thus the Minister for Foreign Affairs, for example, has direct responsibility for Swedish embassies and consulates abroad, and the Minister of Justice is in charge of the enforcement of sections of the Freedom of the Press Act, which is one of the basic laws. Ministers also have authority, by virtue of their office, to see to the general running of their departments: they can thus decide on the details of the division of work within the department, for example. But otherwise they bear no direct official responsibility for administration. The Swedish administrative system is decentralized to a remarkable degree, and a great deal of routine work is hived off from the departments to a whole host of administrative agencies which are legally independent of any outside authority in respect of day-to-day business. This is the explanation of the fact, noted earlier in passing, that the departments are very small-scale units. If the Foreign Office be excepted as a special case, the number of civil servants employed in the other ten departments combined in 1964 totalled less than a thousand, clerical staffs included.[47]

The virtual absence of any general ministerial responsibility for routine administration is a peculiar feature of the Swedish governmental system which dovetails with, and helps to explain, other distinctive pieces of the pattern. It is to be seen, for example, in conjunction with the individual responsibility of civil servants (discussed below in Chapter 5)—an individual responsibility which in turn helps to explain the importance of the Ombudsmen in the scheme of things. It helps to explain the restrictions placed by the constitution upon Parliament's freedom of discussion in respect of administrative matters—not that these restrictions are very important nowadays, but they have been a factor inhibiting the development of the parliamentary question.[48] It has assisted in shaping the main features of Swedish administrative law and, more especially, of the Swedish system of administrative appeals.[49] It may be viewed as a by-product of the decentralized relationship between the departments and the boards.[50]

Are, then, it may be asked, Swedish ministers only responsible collectively? The formal answer, as laid down by the 1809 Constitution and now rescinded, may be briefly looked at first. Swedish ministers were constitutionally responsible, broadly speaking, for the "advice" which they gave to the King in Council. They were regarded by the basic laws as the highest type of civil servant, at the heads of departments whose function it was to prepare business for decision by the King in Council and to execute decisions coming from the King in Council. The elements of myth in all this were obvious, given a modern cabinet system and constitutional mon-

[47] Proposition 1965: 65 (on departmental reform) gives a figure of 842 civil servants for these ten departments plus the Cabinet Office in 1964 (at p. 10). The numbers have increased fairly sharply of late, however, in the wake of the 1965 reforms and are now well over the thousand mark. But the general point remains valid.

[48] See p. 167. [49] See Chapter 6. [50] See the next chapter.

archy, so that the details of the formal rules governing ministerial responsibility need not delay us here.[51] Suffice it to say for the moment that ministerial responsibility was formally tied mainly to the proper "preparation" and execution of business: the point is here that such business was to be formally decided in Council of State and was therefore formally decided collectively—unless some member of the Government minutes his disagreement with the decision, which was hardly in accord with the modern convention.

One might expect ministers, as a result of these arrangements, to be freed from administrative detail and able to concentrate to a large extent on the central tasks of government—defined by the Commission on the Constitution as being "initiating, planning and supervising over the whole field of state activity."[52] This is substantially but not entirely the case. The centre of gravity of departmental work certainly lies in the preparation of larger-scale issues—government Bills, estimates, etc., and the suggestion of norms to be followed by the relevant administrative authorities. The long-term planning function has come more and more to the fore of recent years, as the growth of the departmental sections concerned bears witness.

Nevertheless, it is a fact that no fewer than 38,500 items of business were officially disposed of by the King in Council in 1963, for example.[53] The vast bulk of this is accounted for by small-scale routine business which necessarily has to be settled in reality at departmental level and rubber-stamped higher up. Civil service appointments, resignations and staffing matters generally used to account for a fair percentage of the total. A big bulk now consists of the granting of licences, permits, and dispensations of various kinds—anything from permission to change one's surname to permission to import horses has been reckoned a matter for government decision, and one can even find cases on record of the government granting

[51] The rules may be found in the unrevised RF, articles 9, 13, 15, 38, 106, and 107. More is said about their operation at pp. 158–60.

[52] SOU, 1963: 17, p. 154.

[53] Proposition 1965: 65, p. 10. Foreign Ministry business is excepted from this total as a separate class.

compensation to individuals whose pets have been killed by bears.[54] A good many minutiae continue to come up in the form of administrative appeals. The creation of a Supreme Administrative Court early this century took a considerable load off the government in this last respect, but several categories of administrative appeal still require government attention (including appeals against civil service appointments in certain classified cases).

All of this small-scale business, except appeals, is handled first by the departments and falls into one or other of a number of categories requiring a formal government decision at the end of the day. The departments, which in form prepare it, in reality, as we have seen, decide it: but, since it is largely routine in character, the time and energy of ministers is not greatly engaged and any real processing required is mostly left to the relevant civil servants. Efforts are being made to have as much as possible of this type of business decentralized—as was recommended by the Commission on the Constitution.[55] Compensation questions, for example, have now been farmed out, and a working party has produced over a score of reports to ministers suggesting further measures of decentralization in particular fields.

At times, then, the departments individually, i.e. the ministers individually—make *de facto* decisions on business involving the use of their individual judgement, so that in these instances one may talk of a measure of *de facto* ministerial rule. One may go on to ask the question, How far is it ensured that this element of *de facto* ministerial rule is kept to a necessary minimum and that ministers decide individually only those questions which will not have repercussions beyond their own departments?

The answer to this question involves an assessment of the effectiveness of the arrangements for clearing and co-ordinating government business. The Commission on the Constitution took a critical line about the effectiveness of these arrangements—on the whole, it would seem, an unduly critical line. But its report can still serve as a

[54] Ingelson, *op. cit.*, p. 49. This was in the 1930's, when bears were more common (though still rare).

[55] See below, p. 56.

background to a look at the nature of the relationship between ministers, the Cabinet, and the Council of State.

Arrangements for the Co-ordination of Government Business

Since departments are formally regarded as agencies for preparing business for decision by the King in Council, items are presented in Council by ministers in a traditional order and on the basis of departmental agendas.

> Unless they have a legitimate excuse, all members of the Council shall be present for the consideration of all matters of special importance and magnitude. . . . Such matters are: questions and proposals regarding the adoption of new general laws, the repeal or amendment of those hitherto in force, new general establishments within the various branches of administration, and other questions of a similar character.[56]

Most Council meetings deal with important matters as thus defined, and these will have been debated and settled in cabinet. Council meetings, as we have seen, also dispose of a mass of small-scale business, and in this sense it is true—as the Commission on the Constitution objected—that those taking part have no knowledge of, or interest in, most of the questions coming up for decision. But sessions are quite short, averaging 30–40 minutes, in the course of which between 500 and 1000 items are "decided". They are usually held weekly—as was mentioned earlier—in the Royal Palace in Stockholm on Fridays in the presence of the King—though the frequency tends to drop off in the summer months during what might be called (without any offensive undertones) the national slack season. If there is no important business it is possible to hold a little Council of State for which a quorum of only four ministers is necessary.[56]

Virtually all government business is required by the Constitution to pass through King in Council.[57] Matters of military command in the armed services (*kommandomål*) are the exception, being nominally dealt with in meetings between the Minister of Defence

[56] RF, article 8. [57] *Ibid.*, article 7.

and the King.[58] Minutes were kept in Council by civil servants on a departmental basis, but now one official logs business. The departments provide explanatory sections in government submissions to Parliament ("propositions") couched in the form of speeches supposedly made by their ministers in Council in justification of the relevant measure—fictitious Council minutes, in other words. If these reflected the realities of the situation, as one observer put it in a celebrated comment many years ago, ". . . long before the end nature would have claimed her due and all the members be sound asleep".[59]

It may be agreed that the prodedure in formal Council is highly artificial. The Commission on the Constitution, mindful of its mandate to suggest ways of modernizing the Constitution, accordingly came in with reform proposals. It wanted to decentralize the bulk of business coming to the Council, restricting the Council to the ratification of items with whose final decision the head of State ought to be associated. Among the more important items of this kind may be mentioned government Bills, government messages to Parliament (including, for example, dissolution decisions), top-level civil service appointments, and changes of a permanent character in the organization of government work. All items in these categories would, under the Commission's scheme, have to go from Cabinet to Council for final ratification. By these arrangements the Commission estimated that the volume of business dealt with in Council would be reduced to something of the order of 500 items per year. The Commission also recommended that only ministers with business to transact should be required to attend. It is probable that some slight saving of time would result if these suggestions were to be put into effect, but, given the nature of Council transactions, this would be very marginal. Sweden is not a country where, on the whole, ancient forms are cherished for their traditional value, so that one suspects that the formal Council could not have survived so little

[58] RF., article 15. In fact, the Defence Minister decides these (largely routine) matters, and his written recommendations are formally ratified *ex post* by the King.

[59] "Junius" (Professor Eli F. Heckscher), quoted at Ingelson, *op. cit.*, p. 57.

changed unless it served some useful purpose. In fact it is chiefly valuable as a registration device for government decisions. So far, then, the Commission's recommendations in this sector have met with little favour.

The procedures of the King in Council, on the face of it, suggest the existence of a strong departmentalism. The report of the Commission on the Constitution tends to create the same impression:

> The final decision on almost all business of lesser importance is taken by only one minister and even in questions of greater importance collective decisions . . . are often rather formal in character. . . . Comparison with circumstances in other lands, including our Scandinavian neighbours, results in the decided impression that . . . the collective element in Swedish governmental procedures is notably weak in development.[60]

This certainly hints at a problem of government co-ordination. A little further on in its report the Commission amplified its point in the following words:

> The factors determining whether a particular piece of business shall be submitted to collective consideration in some form or other are chiefly two, namely the formal consideration that the matter concerns more than one department, and the personal judgement of the relevant minister that the opinion of his colleagues must be sought. The formal criterion, however, only partially sifts questions in terms of their importance: some important matters concern only one department, some not so important matters concern several. But, above all, what is termed "collective consideration" is often a pure formality: what happens in many cases is merely that, after an examination chiefly at the civil service level in other departments concerned, the department responsible for the business in question is notified that there is no objection to the proposal. No real consultation occurs between ministers, no real consensus emerges. So far as the second factor determining whether a piece of business shall be considered collectively is concerned—i.e. personal judgement—it nearly always depends solely on the minister who is responsible for taking the final decision on the business. It is often said that a minister soon learns what he can and cannot decide on his own initiative; government work depends on mutual trust and he who neglects to inform his colleagues must reckon with their reactions. In the opinion of the Commission however, there is a wide margin between such a degree of waywardness that colleagues have cause to react and the case where collective consideration is objectively desirable but not required by current practice.

[60] SOU, 1963: 17, pp. 233–4.

> Above all the Commission finds that the present conventions lead to the demand for collective consideration within the government being pitched too low.[61]

The general impression created by this passage is reinforced by a recommendation that the Cabinet should be formally recognized as the place where all the major decisions of government are taken, and that its position in this respect should be strengthened by the enumeration in a special legal document of categories of government business not to be decided by individual ministers. The scope for the exercise of ministerial judgement as to what should or should not be submitted would thereby be reduced—at the same time that the existence of an area of genuine ministerial responsibility would be given formal recognition.

The Commission here, however, seems to have opened itself to the criticisms of under-estimating the effectiveness of the existing arrangements for clearing government business and at the same time of proposing to over-formalize the situation. The arrangements for co-ordinating government business before the King in Council stage are certainly characterized by a rather marked degree of informality, but the informality would seem on balance to be more of an advantage than otherwise. For one thing, a considerable amount of business is transacted—and decisions are taken—at weekday cabinet lunches which ministers are expected to attend whenever possible. Again, departments—contrary to the impression which might be obtained from the Commission report—do in fact transact a great deal of business through conclaves of two, three, or more ministers, so that the load of the Cabinet is correspondingly lightened. (In such cases, each item of business goes on to the Council agenda of the department most concerned with it.)

One specialized variety of smaller inter-departmental conclave attracted the particular fire of the Commission:

> Since no system of government can avoid a rather far-reaching co-ordination of work between the various departments, then in our case—probably in part as a result of the lack of set forms for a common collective consideration of more important government business by the government

---

[61] SOU, 1963:17, pp. 235–6.

> as a whole—a special form of co-ordination has developed the more strongly, viz. co-ordination through the agency of the Finance Department and the Department of Civil Service Affairs. There is hardly cause to examine here the co-ordinating functions of the Department of Civil Service Affairs which spring in large measure from the growth of collective organizations among civil servants and other employees of the state. In the case of the Finance Department it is clear that this Department and its head play, and ought to play, a central role in the work of government. The needs to ensure the unity of the budget, to watch over its development, and to pay attention to the socio-economic aspects of state activity make a co-ordination, and to some extent a control, of the work of the specialist departments a necessary task falling naturally to the Finance Department. The supervisory functions of this Department have, however, of recent years . . . become too closely concentrated on questions of detail, i.e. in fact on technical discussions as to the need for proposed items of expenditure, whereas instead such budgetary discussions should be limited to a consideration of the broad lines of expenditure, within which the more detailed uses of supply should be left as far as possible to the relevant specialist department. The broad lines of expenditure should not be settled in talks between the Finance Department and the relevant specialist department but should come under consideration in a form allowing the participation of the whole Cabinet. A strengthening of the collective element in the work of the Government should therefore also lead to a certain reduction in the co-ordinating and controlling functions of the Finance Department, enabling them to be concentrated on tasks more central to the work of the department.[62]

Concern about a too punctilious scrutiny of financial detail is one thing, and others have criticized the somewhat narrow type of financial control long carried out by the Finance Department.[63] The passage should not be taken to mean, however, that there is no consideration of "the broad lines of expenditure" in Cabinet as things are: it should be taken as part of a general plea for a greater formalization of Cabinet procedure, and as such it is very much open to question.

The Cabinet is, of course, the power-house and co-ordinating centre of the whole governmental machine. Informality of procedure characterizes its meetings, just as rigidity of procedure characterizes formal Council meetings. Cabinet meetings occur as

[62] *Ibid.*, p. 236.

[63] E.g. Heckscher, *op. cit.*, pp. 253–312.

a rule once a week, oftener if business requires it. They are chaired in the absence of the Prime Minister by the Foreign Minister, otherwise by the longest-serving minister. Civil servants are often called upon to introduce business and are apt to be questioned vigorously about it when they have done so. As might be expected, they withdraw before the ministers begin their discussions and before any decisions are taken. All the ministers may be asked consecutively for their individual opinions at times, but votes are not taken. No minutes are kept of the proceedings: ministers may take notes for their private use, but that is all. There is no full formal agenda for these meetings, but (as was mentioned above) a considerable amount of subsidiary work is done at weekday Cabinet lunches which ministers are expected to attend whenever possible. Party political matters can be freely discussed at these lunches: civil servants are not present.[64]

It does not follow from all this that the procedures—or, in this case, the relative lack of them—for the conduct of government business make the co-ordination of government work an unusually difficult task. It is certainly true that the smooth co-ordination of Cabinet work will always depend to a certain extent under any cabinet system on the quality of political judgement possessed by individual ministers as to what should or should not be submitted for collective consideration. The basic difficulties here are universal. There is always the difficulty of assessing whether something which looks like a piece of routine business will turn out to have political repercussions, for example. There is always, too, the difficulty that ministers are busy people who may find it hard to co-operate to the extent that a piece of business demands. But there is little evidence that the informality of Swedish Cabinet procedure puts any special difficulties in the way of co-ordination. There are, indeed, certain built-in safeguards against individual errors of judgement as to whether or not business requires collective consideration in one form or another. Departmental agendas for the King in Council are sent

[64] Gunner Heckscher, *op. cit.*, pp. 212–13; G. Heckscher, Konselj och statsrådsberedning, *Statsvetenskaplig Tidskrift*, 1948, pp. 305–15; Nordenstam, *op. cit.*, pp. 250–1.

to the Prime Minister in advance, so that he is kept posted of what is afoot in the Chancery (as the departments are collectively known). The legal consultants among the Ministers without Portfolio act as a co-ordinating force in ways mentioned earlier in this chapter. Government propositions, draft ordinances, and answers to parliamentary questions and interpellations, moreover, require clearance (or attestation) from all departments before final release.

Summing up, it does not appear that the co-ordination of Cabinet work in Sweden is particularly hampered by faulty procedures or by maverick ministers. Certainly allegations of improper ministerial rule or of faulty co-ordination are not frequent (they are admittedly all but impossible to substantiate). It should, however, be mentioned that there were heated exchanges on this topic in connection with the cessation of aid for certain development projects in Ethiopia in 1962 (the controversy broke out in Autumn, 1963).[65] The same is true of the controversy over the Wennerström spy case.[66] In so far as Sweden has a special problem of co-ordination at Cabinet level, it would appear to result rather from the fact that the administrative system is decentralized. This means that heavy reliance has to be placed on the device of commissions of inquiry since the departments cannot carry out all the work on complex reforms on their own unaided resources—and the co-ordination of the work of these commissions can be a considerable task. Also, a government bent on social reform is bound to want to induce the administrative agencies to move in unison in the same general direction. This automatically involves a special set of co-ordination problems.

One final recommendation of the Commission on the Constitution remains to be considered in this context: the setting up of a Cabinet Office (*Regeringskansli*) with co-ordinating functions. This

[65] The debate was complicated in this instance by being in part concerned with the relationship between a minister and a board. There is some interesting material in *Göteborgs Handels- och Sjöfartstidning*, 25 September 1963.

[66] See Committee on the Constitution, mem. no. 21, 1964. One of the more interesting Press reports on this is to be found in *Nya Wermlandstidningen*, 11 September 1963.

Office, it is proposed, should come under the general jurisdiction of the Prime Minister, on whose behalf it should have the task of carrying out research and inquiry duties. It should watch over the coherence of legislation and of administrative regulations. It should help plan government activity on the parliamentary front. It should finally watch over machinery of government questions, paying special attention to the division of functions between departments and to the possibilities of further decentralization of administrative-type questions from the Chancery. Two Ministers without Portfolio with co-ordinating duties—one legal and one administrative expert—should be attached to it and provided with civil service staffs. The Minister without Portfolio with administrative expertise "should work towards unity within, and a rational organization of, the state administrative system".[67] He should be charged as convenient with the immediate direction of the work of the Office. The Prime Minister's Private Secretary and a Press representative should also be installed there, and additional Ministers without Portfolio might be put in as required. Provision should be made in addition for scientific and technical expertise drawn from the public service to be attached to the Office.

In a Bill presented to the Riksdag in Autumn, 1963,[68] the Government made provision for the creation of an Under-Secretary[69] to serve in what is virtually a Cabinet Office, and in 1964 the post was filled. The new Under-Secretary was to be chiefly concerned with co-ordination questions, notably the progress of government Bills and (initially at least) matters concerning national security. The Office has also been given a press secretary and a legal section under a judge of appeal, and all the signs are that a considerable expansion of its civil service staff will take place to increase planning and co-ordination work (not least the co-ordination of work of commissions of inquiry). The Ministers without Portfolio appointed for

[67] SOU, 1963: 17, p. 225.

[68] Proposition, 1963: 190.

[69] The translation of this official's name (*statssekreterare*) is awkward, but "Under-Secretary" is a reasonably close equivalent and is already in use. See below, pp. 83–86.

their legal expertise are in fact attached to the Cabinet Office, whose lawyers work under their direction.

The Government has also set up an advisory organ for the long-term planning of technical and scientific research reporting to the Cabinet via the Prime Minister as chairman.[70] This advisory body consists of 27 members, 19 of whom are drawn from university staffs (public servants in Sweden); 16 of the 19 are professors—of plasma physics, forestry, genetics, theoretical physics, etc. A smaller working party of 7 was set up at the same time under the Prime Minister's leadership to study questions of importance to the Government in the shaping of research policy.

The Prime Minister and the Dissolution Power

This chapter may be concluded by a glance at one or two other aspects of Cabinet government in Sweden. The terrain here has already been fairly thoroughly charted elsewhere for British readers,[71] and the survey will be restricted to broad outlines—except for a closer look at the very end at the curious rule that continues to debar ministers from appearance in committees of the legislature.

The Swedish Prime Minister normally combines the leadership of the national and the parliamentary parties. He chooses his Cabinet unimpeded by party caucuses.[72] He can dismiss ministers with no more than the normal hazards of politics. He has a certain, rather restricted, right of dissolution. And, in the case of the present Prime Minister, Tage Erlander, there is the additional fact that he is only

[70] This recommendation of the Commission—like, indeed, the plan for a Cabinet Office—was originally mooted in a special report in 1958—SOU, 1958: T14.

[71] See, for example, Rustow, *op. cit.*, chapters 3, 5, and 7, and Andrén, *op. cit.*, *passim*. Elis Håstad, *The Parliament of Sweden*, Hansard Society, London, 1957, contains material of interest in the present context scattered in chapters 4–10 inclusive. Among earlier works of particular value may be cited, N. Herlitz, *Sweden: A Modern Democracy on Ancient Foundations*, University of Minnesota Press, Minneapolis, 1939.

[72] Partial exceptions occurred in 1932 and 1936 (Hansson's first and second governments). E. Håstad, *Partierna i regering och riksdag*, Bonniers, Stockholm, 1949, 2nd rev. edn., p. 11.

the third party leader the Social Democrats have had this century[73] and that he has held the premiership now for an unbroken spell of over 20 years. (He has recently indicated that he intends to resign in the second half of 1969.)

When the leadership of a party falls vacant, both the national executive and the parliamentary party have a hand in the ensuing election. The executive committee of the parliamentary party is strongly represented on the national executive, and is naturally particularly influential there whenever the party is in power. But even so it does not always follow that the parliamentary executive will carry the day. The election of Erlander in 1946 is a case in point: the executive committee of the parliamentary party favoured the candidature of Gustav Möller, who had been a close colleague of the late party leader, Per-Albin Hansson, but the national executive preferred Erlander, and the parliamentary party voting as a whole supported this choice by 94 votes to 72.[74] It may be added that the question of separating the leadership of the national and the parliamentary parties arose on this occasion, and may arise again in the future because of the volume of work involved in the combination of the two offices. The possibility of electing Möller to the chairmanship of the national party was canvassed in 1946 after Erlander had been elected to the leadership of the parliamentary group (and hence, of course, to the premiership), but Möller declined.[75]

The Prime Minister, like most other party leaders, prefers to sit in the Lower House rather than the Upper. Thus Erlander, who was a member of the Upper House when elected to the party leadership, transferred to the Lower at the first opportunity. The two Houses are constitutionally of equal power and authority, the chief differences between them being, firstly, that the Lower is directly and the Upper indirectly elected, and, secondly, that the Lower House

[73] His predecessors were Branting and Hansson. In September 1969 he was succeeded by Palme, as mentioned earlier.

[74] See, for example, O. Nyman, *Parlamentarismen i Sverige*, Ehlins, Stockholm, 1950, p. 97.

[75] Håstad, *Partierna i regering och riksdag*, p. 23.

has the advantage in size (with 233 members as compared with 151 in the Upper House). Ministers may only vote in the House to which they belong, but they have the right to appear and speak in both Houses—even if they do not have a seat in Parliament at all. The fact that Bills are technically discussed simultaneously in both Houses is not always an absolute bar to the exercise of this right, since a slight staggering of time-tables is permissible.

Since the two chambers are constitutionally of equal power and authority, governments are technically responsible to both. This dual responsibility could lead to awkward political situations. General elections to the Lower House normally take place at 4-year intervals; the members of the Upper House are elected for an 8-year term by provincial and other major local councils, and one-eighth retire each year. In the post-war years, however, as we have seen, the Social Democrats have maintained a solid majority in the Upper House, and they have also been able to keep a majority in the Lower House over almost the whole of the same period with the help of intermittent Agrarian and constant Communist support. The difficulty in question will, in any case, be disappearing before long with the introduction of a unicameral system.

It was mentioned earlier that the Prime Minister has a rather limited power of dissolution. Under present arrangements the members of the Lower House sit for a 4-year term. If the House is dissolved, the members returned at the ensuing election can only sit for the remainder of the 4-year term: ordinary general elections must be held in the Autumn of every leap year. The point of this rule is that local elections then normally fall at the mid-point of every Parliament—but, of course, one side-effect is that the Prime Minister is largely deprived of the use of a tactical weapon. There has, in fact, only been one case since 1914 of a "political" dissolution, in 1958, and the next ordinary general election then came along at the usual time 2 years later. The Upper House may also be dissolved, and in this case, too, the newly returned members can only sit for their constituencies for the remainder of the original period—so that some of them could find themselves out again within the year. Since the local councils which elect members of the Upper

House cannot themselves be readily dissolved, the results of an Upper House dissolution are very closely predictable.

Here again, of course, changes are in prospect. General elections to the unicameral legislature will, as already mentioned, fall due every third year and will coincide with local government elections. The Prime Minister will not be able to use his power of dissolution until 5 months after the first meeting of a new legislature, and the ensuing Parliament will only continue to exist for the remainder of the *original* 3-year term. The greater degree of proportionality in the new arrangements for distributing seats will, if anything, strengthen the long-standing tendency for only marginal changes to occur in party representation in Parliament from one election to the next. In short, the Prime Minister will have a right of dissolution even more circumscribed than at present.

A Ministerial Disability

Finally, some reflections on the rule still precariously, and very oddly, surviving from the separation of powers era—the rule that ministers cannot appear before, still less be members of, parliamentary standing committees.[76] There is, for the present, one exception to it: "The Prime Minister, the Minister for Foreign Affairs, as well as, when the nature of the matter under consideration so warrants, any other member of the Council of State, may personally or through a public official communicate verbal or written information to the Foreign Affairs Committee."[77] This particular committee was set up in 1937 with the same membership as the Advisory Council on Foreign Affairs. Since the members of the committee, in their capacity as members of the Advisory Council, were expected generally to be consulted by the Government at the formative stage of any agreements with foreign powers falling to their lot to report on to the Riksdag, it was considered unreasonable to exclude ministers from the meetings of the committee. This did not prevent the more traditionally minded members of the Riksdag from resisting the proposal to allow ministers

[76] RO, article 36, para. 6.

[77] *Ibid.*, article 37, para 2.

entry when the establishment of the committee was under debate,[78] and it was not indeed until 4 years after the committee had been founded that others beside the Minister for Foreign Affairs were granted the privilege.

The rule that ministers shall not appear in committee reflects the ancient determination of the Riksdag to consider questions independently of the influence of the King's nominees. Various attempts were made to lift the prohibition towards the end of the period of minority government in Sweden (1920–32), and in all of them the Social Democratic Party now in power played a prominent part. Individual members of the party tabled motions calling for a reform in 1928 and 1930, and in 1934 the Social Democratic minority government of the day itself produced a bill. Nobody proposed that ministers should be elected to committee or allowed to vote in committee divisions; it was simply intended that they should be able to present information and to state their views. Powerful arguments were advanced in favour of the change. The committees, it was urged, would be able to get a clearer impression of the attitude of the Government by listening to its members than by reading through its highly documented propositions.[79] The only pressures which would be brought to bear on them if ministers were admitted would be the pressures of argument and persuasion—legitimate enough in a democratic state. Finally, it was urged that the reform would do something towards restoring the prestige and the rightful authority of government at a time when governmental weakness was a cause of common concern.

None of these arguments prevailed: the rule still stands. It has, moreover, been maintained by the Social Democrats who formerly opposed it, though since 1936 they have been in a position to abolish it at will. The point is a curious one, though of relatively little importance: it is chiefly of interest for what it turns up by the way. In this case what is turning up is the persistence of the old tradition of *saklighet*. The tradition can be seen operating in an extreme form

[78] FK (Upper House: Första Kammaren) debate, 1937: 37, pp. 3–35. AK (Lower House: Andra Kammaren) debate, 1937: 37, pp. 17–35.

[79] See below, p. 126.

in some of the arguments advanced by those resisting the admission of ministers to committee. Thus, for example, as a member of the Lower House put it in the 1934 debate: "I am apprehensive that the proposed reform will lead to the appearance of a political element which will work to the disadvantage of a purely objective consideration of parliamentary business";[80] or again, this time from the Upper House: "Committees should be as free as possible from the influence of outsiders".[81] These arguments reflect tradition carried to the point of fantasy. Nevertheless, without embarking here on an analysis of the role of the committee in the legislative process,[82] the fact remains that the committees continue to be specialist bodies with a habit of giving close attention to the details of government proposals. They cannot hope to rival the expertise available to the Government; but they afford a useful outlet for the energies of parties spending long years in opposition. There is, however, no doubt but that the ban on the appearance of ministers in committee would have been lifted long ago had it involved governments in anything more than occasional inconvenience. Party loyalties are strong enough to carry a government programme through the legislature in all essentials, and ministers can get information to the committees by informal means if required. There are signs, too, that the critical look which is being taken at the political system as a whole will not leave this corner of it untouched. Certainly the Commission on the Constitution proposed that the ancient ban on ministers in committee should be rescinded.

[80] Herr Lindskog, AK 1934: 37, p. 57.

[81] Herr Sundberg, FK 1934: 35, p. 44.

[82] A short survey of this is given below, pp. 124–8. See also my article The parliamentary role of joint standing committees in Sweden, *American Political Science Review* **45** (1951), 464–73.

CHAPTER 3

Departments and Boards

ORIGINS OF THE DECENTRALIZED ADMINISTRATIVE SYSTEM

The Swedish administrative system, as has been noted, is extremely decentralized. The departments of State, although in fact they handle a fair amount of administrative and quasi-judicial business, are primarily small-scale high-powered planning and policy-making units, and this function, as will be shown, is coming more and more to the forefront. In the nature of the case, however, a good deal of reliance will still have to be placed on commissions of inquiry for working out the details of projected reforms. The dozens of state boards and agencies, ranging in size from what are virtually small committees or councils with a handful of members to concerns such as Swedish Railways with 66,000 employees, are each attached to a particular ministry, but officially they take their orders from the Crown (i.e. the Government as a whole) and not from the ministers. These orders are general in nature and are concerned with matters of policy. They have, however, to be prepared, and each department is at the apex of its own cluster of boards in this connection. In practice, therefore, the way is naturally open for the relevant minister to exercise a considerable amount of influence on decisions taken in the realm of public policy. In matters of day-to-day administration, the boards enjoy a great measure of independence. The general position, then, is to quote the words of a Swedish commentator:

> The King [i.e. the government] through the departments, exercises a general leadership and control over the administration and takes decisions on matters of principle while central boards have an immediate leadership

> and control over special branches of the administration according to the norms set by laws, royal instructions and other directives.[1]

This administrative decentralization has ancient roots, and it has survived various attempts at destruction. The oldest of the state boards, the Exchequer Board (*Kammarkollegium*) dates from the 1530's. The collegial pattern did not become a familiar one in the Swedish administrative system, however, until the reign of Gustavus Adolphus (1611–32), and in its early days it formed an integral part of a centralized administrative structure. Thus the five boards recognized in the Instrument of Government of 1634 were each dominated by one of the five high offices of State—the Lord High Treasurer, the Admiral of the Realm, etc.—and each of these powerful figures was a member of the Council of State. The most powerful of all was the Chancellor, who headed the Chancery (*Kansli*). This was the board which was destined to become the hub of the whole administrative system, for it alone remained central while the others drifted away from royal control. Thus the Instrument of Government of 1720 laid it down that only the President of Chancery among the heads of boards was to sit in the Royal Council, so that the Chancery became the channel for two-way traffic between the Government and the boards, executing government decisions, on the one hand, and presenting business on behalf of the boards, on the other. For these purposes it was divided into a group of offices each dealing with the preparation and execution of business in a particular field and each headed by a secretary. These secretaries for long were inferior in status to the heads of the state boards and did not sit in the Council, so that the heads of the boards preferred to bypass them and take orders only from the King in Council. Not until 1840 were the secretaries permitted to become full members of Council—ministers, in effect—but the boards by then had long enjoyed a strongly independent position and the old arrangement was perpetuated. The present-day departments bear the marks of their origin in the name Chancery by which they are

[1] G. Hesslén, 'Departement och verk', in *Festskrift till Professor Skytteanus Axel Brusewitz*, Uppsala and Stockholm, 1941, pp. 246–63, at p. 247.

still collectively known—though they are no longer quite small enough to be all (except for the Foreign Office) accommodated in the one building.

Not long after the adoption of the present written constitution in 1809, committees of inquiry into the structure of the administration were recommending that the boards be brought under centralized control, but no action was taken. On the contrary, more new boards were created in the course of the century, often by fission from existing ones—the Exchequer Board, in particular, was a prolific source. There was even resistance to the setting up of bureaux for handling specialized blocks of business within the departments—a reform carried through in the 1870's—on the grounds that the centre of gravity in purely administrative matters might thereby shift to the Chancery. The question of abolishing the independence of the boards, never dead, was given another extensive airing early in the present century, when the Liberal Government of Karl Staaff was anxious to put through social welfare legislation unimpeded by what it regarded as bureaucratic conservatism. A committee of inquiry was appointed to investigate the matter in 1908 and it reported in 1912 in favour of organizing the boards as integral parts of the departments. It argued that the decentralization of the administration resulted in circuitousness, delay, and overlapping in the preparation of business; that unified ministerial control was hampered by the independence of the boards; and that the present arrangements had the disadvantage that the experts were in the boards whereas the Government had the responsibility for the final decisions. Similarly, a one-man ministerial inquiry reported in 1917 that the continued independence of the boards threatened the unified control of policy. It is true that up to this period the boards were, as they had long been, the most important agencies for doing the preparatory work on reforms. The suggestion that they should be incorporated, even in a modified way, into the departmental structure, met with powerful opposition from the civil service, largely on the grounds that the traditional independence of the boards was a virtue in itself (an analogy was often drawn between the boards and the courts of law in this connection), and that it helped to keep party politics out. Once again, therefore, the project for centralizing the administrative structure came to nothing. During the present century the number of boards has increased considerably, and the agitation for incorporating them into departments has died down—along with complaints about bureaucratic conservatism. The past 3 years, for example, have seen the creation of new boards dealing with nature conservancy and traffic safety, and also the amalgamation of the old Social Welfare Board with the Board of Health in a large new unit. It occasionally happens that a new category of business—civil aviation, for example—is initially administered by a department, but this is an interim arrangement, and the practice is for such questions to be moved out to boards before long.

The success of the boards in resisting centralization can be explained partly in terms of historical and cultural factors, partly on functional grounds. The earlier attempts at centralization were made at a time when Parliament itself was heavily penetrated by civil servants and when the bureaucracy was a powerful elite within the state (the position may be contrasted with that in Britain in Chadwick's day). Probably even more important was the pervasiveness of the tradition that administration was an activity requiring close formal control by rules and regulations so that the liberties of the subject should not be overthrown in the perennial quest for efficiency. The importance of lawyers in the Swedish public service is examined further in the next chapter, and perhaps meantime the point might be made that ministers themselves were in these early days regarded as properly limited and checked by much the same legal restrictions as other servants of the state. With the advent of parliamentary government this latter consideration was naturally greatly weakened in force, but the old norms were still held valid in the administrative sphere. Again, the days of the social pre-eminence of the bureaucracy have passed, but value continues to be attached to the principle that a measure of public discussion should occur between experts and politicians before public policy is shaped, and this factor (which is discussed further in Chapter 5) has helped to buttress the independence of the boards. This last point may be viewed also as a functional advantage of a decentralized system, and to it may be added the consideration that decentralization has the powerful further advantage of helping to free the central departments for the important function of long-term policy planning.

An idea of the range and diversity of boards and agencies may be obtained from a brief glance at some of those currently attached to the departments of Finance and of the Interior. The Finance Department stands at the head of a particularly rich crop, among them the following: (a) the *Excise Board* (*Kontrollstyrelsen*): exercises a general surveillance over the manufacture of alcoholic drinks and over the state wines and spirits monopoly; administers a wide variety of indirect taxes; keeps a national register of drunkenness offences. (b) The *Customs Board* (*Generaltullstyrelsen*). (c) The *Organization and Methods Office* (*Statskontoret*): the work of this agency is discussed in Chapter 6 below and is closely allied with that of (d), the *National Audit Office* (*Riksrevisionsverket*), which is discussed at the same stage. (e) The *Tax Appeals Court* (*Kammarrätten*): an important part of the structure of administrative courts in Sweden. (f) The *Public Works Office* (*Byggnadsstyrelsen*): co-ordinates work in the sphere of town planning besides carrying out state building projects and acting as a common service unit in respect of fuel use in public offices, etc. (g) The *Mint and Assay Office* (*Mynt och justeringsverket*). (h) The *Central Statistical Office* (*Statistiska centralbyrån*). (i) The *Banks Inspectorate* (*Bankinspektionen*). (j) The *Insurance Inspectorate* (*Försäkringsinspektionen*). (k) The *Economic Research Institute* (*Konjunkturinstitutet*): analyses trends in the national economy and produces the national income figures. Works closely with the Central Statistical Office. (It should be added that some of these units seem likely to be transferred to the new Department of Industrial Affairs.)

Among the boards attached to the Department of the Interior are: (a) the *Housing Board* (*Bostadsstyrelsen*) supervises the administration of state loans and subsidies in aid of housing programmes—the bulk of the actual administration being carried out by provincial housing commissions and by local government authorities; hears appeals against decisions of the subordinate authorities in this field; assists local government authorities with their housing plans; carries out research into house-building techniques and disseminates the results;

keeps statistics of house building, loans, etc. (b) The *Labour Court* (*Arbetsdomstolen*): as the name implies, a specialized judicial authority. Chiefly concerned with disputes relating to the interpretation of collective agreements; also handles cases concerning illegal industrial disputes. It is a court of final instance in these and a number of other types of case of lesser importance and frequency. (c) The *Labour Market Board* (*Arbetsmarknadsstyrelsen*): supervises labour exchanges and acts as a national information centre on employment opportunities; supervises (through a specialized sub-section) unemployment insurance schemes; deals with the training and employment of handicapped persons; administers state grants towards industrial retraining, the encouragement of a mobile labour force, etc., and is concerned with location of industry questions and regional economic planning; draws up (through another specialized sub-section) forecasts of trends in the labour market and administers measures designed to counter seasonal and cyclical unemployment; carries out research projects and keeps statistics in its field.

It will be evident from these examples that most boards are engaged in largely routine business in uncontroversial sectors. Some, such as the Housing and the Labour Market Boards (the latter, in particular, is something of an exception to this general rule), act as the head agencies for a whole network of their own provincial or regional organizations. The boards generally are intended to deal with the day-to-day aspects of public business while the departments concentrate on the wider political issues—but, of course, policy suggestions can arise out of administrative experience. Thus the boards are expected, where appropriate, to keep abreast of technical developments in their own fields and to make proposals for change when their professional expertise indicates this to be necessary. Early in 1967, for instance, the Labour Market Board successfully proposed to the Government that it should release moneys from its investment funds to counteract the effects of slackening industrial investment. The boards generally are also expected to criticize objectively and in the light of their specialist knowledge the measures which are circulated to them for their formal opinion. Nevertheless, some boards may occasionally find themselves involved in controversy as the result of enjoying a wide discretionary power or of discovering that an apparently administrative issue may have political implications—as, for example, the original Overseas Aid Commission (*Nämnden för internationellt bistånd*) found in its day.[2]

A number of questions come to mind at this point. Firstly, how does a government bent on putting through reforms succeed in inducing the decentralized administrative agencies to move at the desired speed and in the desired direction? Secondly, how do the departments, with the relatively slender staffs at their disposal, manage to cope with the complex tasks involved in planning and legislating for social change under modern conditions? Thirdly, what is the practical significance today of the decentralized administrative system?

Extent and Methods of Central Control

The general framework for government control of the administration is provided by "the norms set by laws, royal instructions and other directives" not least, financial directives and the regulation of establishments, etc., through control of supply. The legislative process is unusual enough to warrant separate treatment,[3] but it is relevant here to say that the heavy reliance on commissions of inquiry—and the increasing reliance on departmental inquiries—have ensured that the boards no longer enjoy their old predominance at the preparatory stage of legislation. The ways in which general rules hedge in the boards from the founding statute onwards are many and various, as one would expect. Thus state loans and grants for a particular social purpose may be reserved to the Government when they exceed a stipulated figure while the relevant administrative agency is allowed to handle loans and grants below that figure —as in the case of aid to industry to induce it to locate itself in the desired places, which a 1964 government Bill[4] vests in the Labour Market Board in respect of the lesser sums, but only subject to detailed

[2] E.g. *Göteborgs Handels- och Sjöfartstidning*, 25 September 1963.

[3] See Chapter 5. [4] Proposition, 1964: 185.

supplementary regulations. It should be added that administrative agencies generally are expected to pay regard to the statements of purpose accompanying all propositions, commission reports, and, to a certain extent, the reports of parliamentary standing committees. They are, in other words, expected to administer according to the spirit of the laws and not just the letter.

The "royal instructions" mentioned above denote the Instructions issued by the Government to regulate the administrative structure and functioning of most of the boards. These Instructions are virtually little constitutions, specifying, for example, what the voting procedure shall be on the board concerned, what functionaries shall be responsible for the preparation of business, and in what form minutes are to be kept. Sometimes they charge the relevant board specifically with the duty of promoting research and advance in its particular sector of the administration. They are supplemented by a General Instruction for Administrative Agencies (*Allmänna verksstadgan*), currently dating from 1955, which contains rules designed to unify practice in connection with a miscellany of matters including, for example, disciplinary questions and interview times for visitors. It must be added that the Instructions for particular boards are, like so many written constitutions, often imperfect guides to practice. The Rules of Procedure (*Arbetsordningar*) issued by many boards themselves within the framework of Instructions are usually more reliable sources.[5]

The Constitution lays down a general obligation for administrative authorities to "perform their duties and functions in accordance with the instructions, rules and regulations already issued or which may hereafter be issued" and to "obey the King's orders and commands". But, as the Commission on the Constitution observed in its report:

> Article 47 of the Instrument of Government [i.e. the article laying down the obligation] was not intended to breach the Swedish legal tradition according to which administrative authorities in certain fields

---

[5] Heckscher, *op. cit.*, pp. 35–36, gives some examples.

shall be independent and have the same right and duty to obey the dictates of their own judgement as the courts of law. This principle is a characteristic feature of Swedish administration. It is interconnected with the principle that, in contrast to the rule in sundry foreign lands, every civil servant is punishable for his decisions, while, on the other hand, the parliamentary responsibility of the Government does not stretch to the decisions of subordinate authorities. It is not possible to pin down in a general formula how far the independence of administrative authorities extends.[6]

Some generalizations may nevertheless be made. Firstly, the decentralized authorities are usually jealous of their independence within the framework set by formal prescription—and, it may be added, of financial controls, of which more will be said shortly. Secondly, that framework may be set narrowly or widely—to some extent depending on the sector (in defence matters, for example, the Government often exercises a comparatively detailed control), to some extent again depending on the performance of the authority concerned. Thirdly, and connected with the second point, the more judicially the authority is acting, the more complete its freedom—as one might expect. A certain amount of control over practice in this field can be obtained by the Government when cases come up to it on appeal.

Again, the constitutional duty laid on administrative authorities to obey "instructions, rules, and regulations" technically signifies an obligation to obey general directives, while the duty to "obey the King's orders and commands" signifies an obligation to obey directives in particular cases. In both cases, the directives in question are directives formally promulgated in the name of the Government as a whole. But, in the words of an authoritative legal commentator:

> It certainly does not happen nowadays that the King [=Government] gives formal written official orders [i.e. in individual cases] of the type envisaged. When a certain administrative measure is considered desirable, the possibility is, of course, open of trying to induce the relevant civil servant to adopt it by approaching him orally. In such a case, however, the responsibility for the official act rests completely with the civil servant taking the decision.[7]

---

[6] SOU, 1963: 17, pp. 254–5.

[7] R. Malmgren, *Sveriges grundlagar*, 6th edn., Norstedt, Stockholm, p. 52.

We are here on ground that has certain affinities with, and is as politically sensitive as, the twilight zone in minister–public corporation relationships in Britain. A considerable volume of informal two-way traffic goes on in particular sectors between ministers and under-secretaries, on the one hand, and the heads of boards attached to their departments, on the other—some of it by telephone and some by informal talks.[8] Consultation between administrative authorities in the same field is natural and, indeed, almost inevitable. One has to distinguish, however, between the issuing of underhand directives—which is always improper—and the giving of advice on particular complex cases. Ministers may, for instance, telephone advice in view of the possible political repercussions of some administrative action. Informal inquiries may be made in connection with some complaint about board action. But circumspection is forced on departments in the nature of the case: we come back to the point that boards are jealous of their independence in the areas where they have legal responsibility.

The control of the decentralized sector by financial means is one of the most effective devices which the Government has for ensuring that its will prevails. The Finance Department occupies the key position within the Chancery in this respect, as one might expect, assisted by some other agencies which also have duties in the field, notably the Organization and Methods Office. The subject is a large one, and for the sake of balance—and also because a good account exists already in English[9]—the essentials only will be sketched here.

Every administrative agency has to have its estimates passed with government approval. For this purpose a state board with regional offshoots, for example, has to collect the estimates of these local administrations and forward them together with its own every September to the Government via the relevant departments (e.g. the Housing Board sends in estimates to the Department of the

[8] Instances of kinds of two-way traffic are given in Heckscher, *op. cit.*, pp. 240–3. On the general issue, see B. Wennergren, Förvaltnings forfarandet i ärenden angående enskilda, in Andrén *et al.* (ed.), *Svensk statsförvaltning i omdaning*, at pp. 66–67.

[9] N. Andrén, *Modern Swedish Government*, chapter 9.

Interior from the provincial housing boards which come under its general jurisdiction). The relevant department is not passive in the matter but usually carries out some pruning before starting the annual higgling process with the Finance Department once the other interested financial agencies have had their say. This, of course, is one point at which a minister who is at loggerheads with a board attached to his department can carry the day.

These considerations apply with particular force to the state boards which are primarily administrative in character. They only apply in much diluted form to the boards carrying out business activities—the trading agencies (*affärsverk*). These are the giants in the decentralized sector—the Post Office, the Telecommunications Board (*Televerket*), the State Railways (*Statens järnvägar*—SJ), the Civil Aviation Board (*Luftfartsstyrelsen*), the Hydro-Electric Board (*Vattenfallsstyrelsen*), the Crown Lands Board (*Domänstyrelsen*), and the Defence Supplies Board (*Försvarets fabriksverk*).[10] These agencies have to submit their annual estimates just like all the others, but in practice they are allowed a much larger degree of autonomy on their budgets and in their staffing policy. So far as the current budgets are concerned, expenditure is expected to be met out of trading receipts, and though any surplus has to be surrendered to the Exchequer, the boards are entitled to overspend their estimates without requiring government sanction. Under these circumstances, the approval of estimates by the Government becomes something of a formality except that it enables the Government to keep an eye on the general trading position. Control over investment budgets was relaxed in 1962 as part of a reform designed to allow these boards more autonomy: the present arrangements are that, in general, a block annual authorization is made for the investment purposes of each board, and, though every board has to itemize its requests, transfers between items are freely allowed to meet contingencies. No independent borrowing is permitted. Prices and tariffs are, moreover, generally fixed by the Government, not by the boards—postal charges (meaning in practice chiefly letter rates) are

[10] The Civil Aviation and the Defence Supplies boards can be excepted from the "giant" category.

traditionally formally settled by Parliament. There has been agitation of recent years for the conversion of the trading agencies into state companies, which are not a part of the public service. But this has steadily been resisted, chiefly because of the regard which has to be paid to social and defence considerations in this sector of the economy. The 1962 reforms are to be seen against this background. Trading agencies, finally, are allowed considerably more freedom than the more purely administrative boards in the matter of appointing staffs. But even so they are considerably less free than state companies in this regard.

> Because of the rigid pay structure [to cite a Swedish commentator] the boards can have difficulty in attracting and keeping qualified personnel in fields where there is stiff competition from the private sector. Unlike the [state] companies the boards in general are not able to raise an employee's pay for the job. An increase in salary has often to be engineered by promoting the person concerned from the position he has and where perhaps he fits best.[11]

The conditions attaching to grants given to administrative boards, in particular, help to decide the amount of autonomy they enjoy. Three general categories of grant can be distinguished: project grants (*förslagsanslag*), earmarked grants (*reservationsanslag*), and undesignated grants (*obetecknade anslag*). Project grants are for purposes which can only approximately be costed. They may, therefore, be exceeded—but the purposes for which, and terms on which, they may be used are tightly regulated. They are much resorted to, for example, in meeting social welfare expenditure. Earmarked grants may not be overspent, but any surplus remaining after one financial year may be held over and used in the next without special authorization being required. Undesignated grants are tied rigidly to the budgetary year for which they are given and may not be exceeded. They account for about 1 per cent of the budget authorizations, while project grants account for about five-sixths. It should be added that the sums voted by the Riksdag, with conditions attached,

[11] Arne Brodd, Företagsformer, in Andrén *et al.*, *op. cit.*, pp. 195–215, at p. 212. See also D. V. Verney, *Public Enterprise in Sweden*, Liverpool University Press, 1959, pp. 37–40, 70–71.

stand at the disposal of the Government. The Government then issues directive letters (*regleringsbrev*) to the several parts of the administrative system, specifying in still greater detail how precisely the moneys are to be used. The flexibility of budgetary regulation, and its impact upon board autonomy, may be illustrated by a few extracts from the report of the 1960 Commission of Inquiry into the Labour Market Board. The Labour Market Board, not least by virtue of its power to encourage industrial mobility, has been one of the most important of all the decentralized agencies.

> The *shape* of labour market policy is governed by statutes or royal regulation. . . . The *scope* of labour market policy is decided by the grants voted by the Riksdag for each budgetary year. . . . Grants are usually tied to specified limited purposes, but can in certain cases be used for alternative measures. This is true, for instance, of the big grant for Public Works, etc., from which moneys can be freely drawn not only for public works purposes but also for economic aid to workers on the move. The possibility of using voted moneys for alternative ends is to be viewed as a recognition of the fact that various routes can often be taken when attacking problems of balance in the labour market . . . one . . . cannot foretell with sufficient accuracy . . . the need for labour market policy measures. This has given rise to technical budgetary arrangements giving a certain insurance against unforeseen events. Thus a percentage of the grants at the disposal of the Labour Market Board are project grants. . . . By amalgamating several larger or smaller grants in aid of different activities to cover groups of measures which can be resorted to as alternatives, the LMB has of recent years been successively given increased freedom of action in certain fields. . . . In the opinion of the inquiry, this freedom of action must not only be maintained but also . . . increased in order that both public works and the grants designed to aid geographical mobility may continue to be flexible and effective instruments in an active labour market policy. From this point of view the inquiry regrets the limitation of the freedom of action of the board imposed with effect from the 1964/5 budgetary year in respect of projects in the field of tourism and outdoor activities which signifies that every item of business of this kind shall be submitted for royal approval.[12]

The problem has now to be considered of the extent to which the administration can be said to be politicized. For the moment, in the context of an analysis of the means by which the Government gets

[12] SOU, 1965: 9, *Arbetsmarknadspolitik*, pp. 485–8.

the decentralized sector of the administration to move in the direction it wishes, the discussion will be confined to the state boards and the provincial governments: the departments will be examined later.

The key positions so far as the boards are concerned are the director-generalships at the top. These are filled at the discretion of the Government, normally on the proposal of the relevant minister, for a fixed term—6 years is the usual period. Reappointment on the expiry of the term is the rule. One Swedish commentator records that "the heads of the boards themselves are nowadays persons who have got their training and outlook primarily as politicians";[13] another concludes that "political qualifications have very little scope".[14] The former would appear to be more accurate if referring to the inter-war period, when the recruitment of career politicians to director-generalships was commoner than is the case now. Even so, the recruitment of persons with a political background was never a universal rule: for one thing, many of the boards are scientific and technical in character and require to be headed by specialists in the field, so that internal promotion of career civil servants is common in these instances. Thus, for example, the Director-General of the Defence Research Institute (*Försvarets forskningsanstalt*) was listed in 1965 as an aeronautical engineer with previous service in that establishment, the Director-General of the Board of Health (*Medicinalstyrelsen*)[15] was a doctor with a distinguished professional record, and the Director-General of the Land Commission (*Lantmäteristyrelsen*) was a surveyor promoted internally after a brief spell as acting head of the Ordnance Survey Board (*Rikets allmänna kartverk*). Evidence of the recruitment of "persons who have got their training and outlook primarily as politicians" is scanty. Thus a survey of a cross-section of forty-seven boards and agencies listed

[13] G. Hesslén, *Den svenska förvaltningen*, Stockholm, Bonniers, 3rd edn., 1956, p. 29.

[14] O. Nyman, Rekryteringen till verkschefsposterna, *Statsvetenskaplig Tidskrift*, 1964, pp. 317–35, at p. 328.

[15] This board has now been merged into the powerful Social Welfare Board (*Socialsstyrelsen*).

in the *1965 State Calendar* revealed only two clear cases of the appointment of politically aligned persons.[16] Only one of these had been in Parliament—and since he was the Conservative at the head of the Defence Supplies Board this would seem to be a reflection of the traditional right-wing interest in military matters rather than evidence of politicization in the usual sense. The other case was the Social Democratic ex-editor at the head of the Housing Board who had earlier had a spell of service at the Labour Market Board. The figure of two is, however, almost certainly too low: some six or seven directors-general had been identified in the opposition press at one time or another as openly Social Democratic in sympathy, for example.[17] One also finds the occasional director-generalship held by ex-officials of LO (the Swedish equivalent of the TUC)—e.g. in 1965 this held true of the Labour Protection Board (*Arbetarskydds-styrelsen*) and of the Highways and Waterways Board (*Väg- oc-vattenbyggnadsstyrelsen*). It should be said, of course, that no director-generalship is a sinecure, and appointments cannot be made just for services rendered to the labour movement or party without the risk of exposure and consequent damage to government credit. Isolated cases have occurred of political nominees turning out to be incompetent, but they are very few and far between. The rule is to appoint men of proven administrative ability and experience in public affairs.

There is a fair amount of circulation of personnel in Sweden from the courts of law to the administration (and, to some extent, back again), and also from one sector of the administration to another in the upper reaches. Thus highly qualified lawyers—who are usually though not always politically uncommitted—are not infrequently appointed to director-generalships; examples in the 1965 lists include the heads of the new Police Board (*Rikspolisstyrelsen*) and of the Exchequer Board, both of whom had been judges in courts of appeal

[16] The information about heads of boards, etc., is drawn from the 1965 *State Calendar*, from *Vem är Vem* and from *Vem är Det*, these last two being Swedish equivalents of *Who's Who*.

[17] E.g. *Göteborgs Handels- och Sjöfartstidning*, "Politiska ämbetsmän", 15 February 1965. It would be rash to regard this evidence as conclusive.

before gaining administrative experience in the departments and then moving out to the decentralized sector of the administration. Movement from the departments to the headship of boards is, indeed, quite common. In many cases the civil servants thus transferred are apolitical career officials, but sometimes they are known to be members of the Social Democratic Party or open sympathizers with its policies. This last is especially, but by no means universally, true of ex-under-secretaries, at least nine of whom according to the 1965 lists held director-generalships—though as it happens almost all of this particular group were clearly apolitical. The position of under-secretaries will be analysed more closely in connection with the structure of departments. Meanwhile the general situation may be summed up by saying that while no government will readily appoint known opponents to the headships of politically sensitive boards, the number of persons appointed having an obvious political affiliation to the ruling party remains quite small. This large sector of the administration is not, on the whole, politicized.[18a]

Proportionately many more politicians are appointed to provincial governorships: a check on the 1965 lists revealed that 9 out of the 24 had actively supported the Social Democrats in one capacity or another, and this is if anything a modest estimate. The fact that a further 5 (at least) had been active politicians in the ranks of opposition indicates, however, that there is no spoils system at work here either. Ten (some with political affiliations) had been under-secretaries in the departments. The office of Provincial Governor can be exacting (provincial governments have a vast range of duties) and is always dignified, being traditionally "the King's eye" in the locality. It is included here because, despite this last fact, the legal position of provincial governments is analogous to that of state boards, and they enjoy a similar degree of autonomy. There was long something of a convention that distinguished opposition politicians were, when appointed to provincial governorships, appointed to provinces of a similar political complexion. In 1963, however, the ex-leader of the Conservative Party was given the governorship of Gävleborg, a strongly Social Democratic province.

[18a] Nyman, *op. cit.*, gives a systematic and careful analysis.

It need hardly be added that the office is not to be exercised in a partisan manner.

It was said earlier that administrators are expected to act according to the spirit of the laws. Conflict situations are rare, even though many individual civil servants may find themselves at times privately out of sympathy with a particular government policy. Open political-type conflict has virtually died out, but there is always the risk of it in the event of a change of government. Again, it occasionally—decreasingly often—happens that a civil servant from a board is elected to the Riksdag and finds himself crossing political swords with his minister.[18b] But this is really little to the purpose, because administrative obstruction would be unlikely to follow political combat. Another occasional type of conflict situation is where a government is anxious to implement reforms and finds that an agency concerned in their administration is not administering them in the way the Government would like.

One device for use in connection with difficulties of this kind is indicated by Heckscher in his panoramic survey of the Swedish administration: "When there is a clash between the government and the head of a board, the possibility of sacking him and appointing another in his stead is almost never exploited in our country. But occasionally the result is that the settlement of all the more important questions is shifted to the department instead."[19] Or, again, boards may be transferred from one departmental area to another with consequent gains or losses of power. The more readily available remedy, however, is to use the weapon of altering the conditions under which supply is granted.

So much, then, for the means by which the Government induces the decentralized administration to move towards the desired goals at the desired speed. Alongside them a series of what might be called legality checks provide reinforcement. These checks include the hearing of administrative appeals and the legal rules governing the responsibilities of individual civil servants. These are best considered

[18b] The subject of civil servants in politics in Sweden is discussed further in Chapter 5.

[19] Heckscher, *op. cit.*, p. 233.

separately later (in Chapter 6). Finally, it should be said that ministers have a general power to require information from the decentralized sector of the public service in connection with their preparation of government business. But, of course, the normal condition of government–board relations is one of harmony, not of conflict. The analysis just given is primarily to be read as a study of the ways in which coherence is imposed on a structure which could easily become chaotic, but which in practice functions with very little friction.

The Departments of State

At this point it is time to survey the central part of the administration, the departments of State, otherwise known as the Chancery. There are, as was mentioned, twelve departments in Sweden: Justice, Foreign Affairs, Defence, Social Welfare, Communications, Finance, Education, Agriculture, Commerce, Interior, Civil Service Affairs, and Industrial Affairs (this last just newly created). The number is fixed by statute. The division of labour within the framework thus set may be rearranged as required by means of administrative regulations. Thus, for example, within the past few years merchant-shipping questions have been moved from the Department of Commerce to the Department of Communications so as to leave the former freer for the increasingly heavy burden of international trading problems; lotteries, many of which are held in Sweden for educational and cultural ends, have been shifted from Commerce to Education; and labour market questions have gone from the Social Welfare Department to the Department of the Interior because of their importance for local government and for the location of industry, which was already being handled by the latter ministry. A major reorganization of functions carried out in 1967 was submitted for parliamentary approval at the same time as the increase in the numbers of Ministers without Portfolio. The most significant changes were the expansion of the functions of the Finance Department to include the tasks previously allocated to the Department of Commerce on the domestic economic front and the transfer of local and provincial government business from the Department of the Interior to the Communications Department.

Most departments have a cluster of state boards attached to them. The Foreign Office was for long exceptional in not having any agencies within its orbit, being itself both a department and an administrative authority in its own right, but it was recently given care of the board in charge of the administration of overseas aid (now known as SIDA—Swedish International Development Agency).[20]

In 1965 the Government put through a measure[21] reorganizing the traditional structure of the departments of State with the purpose of improving their efficiency as staff agencies planning and shaping government policy. The bulk of the routine administration is to continue to be carried out by the state boards, and most of the preparatory work for reforms will continue to be handled by the commissions of inquiry. The reorganization should, however, enable the ministries to adjudicate better on the voluminous material coming in from inquiries, on remit, and in the form of estimates.

Before this time most departments—a notable exception being the Foreign Office—had been organized on a dualistic basis. The politically significant aspects of their work were carried on in a special division or divisions (occasionally subdivided into bureaux) under the supervision of an Under-Secretary. It was here, for example, that the terms of reference of commissions of inquiry within the ambit of the department were drafted for Cabinet consideration; that the work on the preparation of estimates was done; and that other parliamentary business was handled (propositions, answers to questions, action on requests coming from the Riksdag, etc.). Experts were often drafted in on a temporary basis from other sectors of the administration, and party members with specialized knowledge were drafted in temporarily from outside, in order to help out on the Under-Secretary's front. The more purely admini-

[20] For a fuller list of department-board links, see N. Andrén, *Modern Swedish Government*, pp. 115–19.

[21] Proposition, 1965: 65.

strative work was carried on in another set of divisions and bureaux under the general supervision of the Permanent Secretary (*Expeditionschef*), whose responsibility was (and is) to ensure coherence and co-ordination in this field. Alongside this main pattern most departments in addition had a legal division under a Chief Law Officer, staffed chiefly from the courts and largely concerned with the drafting of Bills in collaboration with the Under-Secretary's division. The preparation of cases for the Supreme Administrative Court (*Regeringsrätt*) is also handled by legally qualified staffs within the relevant departments.[22]

The new structure marks the end of the arrangement whereby the sub-units of the department under their respective official heads worked in parallel with each other. The three main officials in each department—the Under-Secretary, the Permanent Secretary, and the Chief Law Officer, with the Under-Secretary still taking precedence—are to exercise their traditional functions over the whole area of the department. The old sub-units are in general to be integrated and rearranged to correspond to blocks of business rather than to the nature of the work. In this way it is hoped that the expertise in particular fields will be concentrated rather than split; that the fruits of administrative experience will be brought to bear more closely on policy planning; and that at the same time administrative work will be carried out more consciously in the light of government policy. The new structure is also designed to be more flexible than the old, with one civil servant (the *huvudman*) in charge of each block of business under the supervision of the triumvirate at the top and with the possibility of one side within each unit relieving the other when the pressure of work is high (in practice it has been the Under-Secretary's side of the department which has tended to have the worst spells of congestion in the past).

The reform also provides for a Planning and Budget Office in each department to co-ordinate the various blocks of business within it and to prepare the estimates. A number of departments had already instituted special planning units—the Department of Education, for example, had a working group on long-term planning, and

[22] See Chapter 6.

the Department of Commerce had an industrial division which, among other things, co-ordinated power policy. The reform widens and deepens the trend, making it clear at the same time that the secondment of experts at need from other branches of the administration for temporary service in a department is to continue (as no doubt will the *ad hoc* importation of party men). The legal divisions are to remain (renamed Legal Offices): the Chief Law Officer, working in conjunction with his two top-level colleagues, is more clearly given a primary responsibility for draft legislation. An International Affairs Office is to be created in departments with a heavy load of international business. Finally, it is recognized that one or two departments—such as Finance—will require variants of the general blueprint. (Finance will employ more senior civil servants than any of the others.)

The Under-Secretary of a Swedish department, as has been indicated, is much concerned with the shaping and execution of policy, whereas the Permanent Secretary is traditionally the apolitical administrator. It is regarded as nothing out of the way in Sweden if the former is an active sympathizer with the government party: in some cases, therefore, it would be fair to say that the kind of work done by a British Permanent Secretary is done in Sweden by a party man. In the event of a change of government, some under-secretaries would be very liable to be changed also—despite the fact that a fair number of them are politically uncommitted career civil servants: permanent secretaries would expect to stay at their posts. Furthermore, the turnover among under-secretaries is high even without a government change. The work-load is exceptionally heavy and the usual span of office is 5 or 6 years—though spells of 12 years or so are not unknown. There is a marked tendency, too, for younger men to be employed. Two of the twelve under-secretaries listed in the *1965 State Calendar* were over 50 (counting among the twelve the Under-Secretary to the Cabinet Office and also the Privy Secretary to the Department of Foreign Affairs—this last being a late eighteenth-century office of equivalent status but distinctive character): the ages of the other ten varied between 38 and 46, and the overall average was 44·7. After their spell of duty is over, under-secretaries move out to other sectors of the administration—a number, as was shown earlier, become heads of state boards, while some become provincial governors and some, indeed, enter the Government. Permanent secretaries, on the other hand, are often the senior men (by age) of the partnership, and though they occasionally move out to take over, for example, the director-generalship of a board, they more usually stay put.

A commission of inquiry into entry qualifications for the public service recorded in its report that "a thorough acquaintance with various social problems and with the political conditions [necessary] for their solution is . . . often of great importance"[23] for those working on the policy-planning side of a department. A political commitment may well be regarded as a help here. The present Minister of Commerce, for example, Gunnar Lange, had earlier filled the crucial under-secretaryship at the Finance Ministry from 1950 to 1954 and was Under-Secretary at the Department of Agriculture for a spell before that. Similarly, Krister Wickman, the Minister without Portfolio with special responsibility for economic affairs (now designated to lead the new Department of Industrial Affairs), had been Under-Secretary of the Finance Department for some years. Again, Ingvar Carlsson, a Social Democrat MP, was appointed Under-Secretary to the Cabinet Office in autumn, 1967. This latter is a position which one would expect to be filled by a man in tune with government policy, and Carlsson replaced a former Under-Secretary to the Department of Agriculture who had been a councillor in the Social Democratic interest on the Lidingö council and who now moved out to become the Director-General of the new Nature Conservancy Board. There are gradations of political commitment until one comes to the politically neutral career civil servant and/or lawyer. Thus, for example, the Under-Secretary at the Defence Department had earlier been a party official in the Södermanland branch of the Social Democratic Party, while the Under-Secretary to the Civil Service Affairs Department had had a long spell as chairman of the SDP Youth League. The Privy Secretary at the Foreign Office had earlier been Ambassador to the

[23] SOU, 1953: 15, *Juridisk och samhällsvetenskaplig utbildning*, p. 29.

German Federal Republic and, before that again, a Social Democratic editor—incidentally illustrating the fact that Swedish ambassadors include a sprinkling of politically aligned men (and women).[24] Alongside the politically inclined under-secretaries there are always a number of apoliticals. The under-secretaryship to the Department of Justice is one of the likeliest to fall into this category and is usually held by a high-ranking lawyer (at present by a former judge in a court of appeal).

The extent of political involvement at the level of under-secretary—six or seven of the total number may be reckoned as politically committed—is an occasional source of complaint in the opposition Press. A common riposte is the inquiry whether Social Democratic under-secretaries were employed when the Liberals and Conservatives were in power in the 1920's.[25] It is clear that this central sector of the administration is noticeably more politicized than the decentralized zone, especially when account is taken of the fact that the Under-Secretary's side of the department sometimes contains a sprinkling of staff with a clearly political background. It is also true that the Swedish civil servant, for reasons to be analysed later,[26] does not have to be divorced from politics in the same sense as his British counterpart. Nevertheless, the highly political type of under-secretary and his political aides—where these occur—are best regarded as injections into a service which has never been subject to a spoils system—or not, at least, since the eighteenth century.

Since the Under-Secretary's side of a department is so much concerned with parliamentary business, it is not surprising that the burdens on it fluctuate markedly in harmony with the parliamentary year. The pressure of work in connection with the preparation of Bills, etc., is heaviest just before the Riksdag opens, and again in the early Spring before the expiry of the time-limit for their submission. Contact has also to be kept during parliamentary sessions

[24] Not always Social Democrats—e.g. the appointment of Gunnar Heckscher (Conservative) as Ambassador to India.

[25] See, for example, *Smålands Folkblad*, 20 March 1964.

[26] Chapter 4.

with the secretariats of Riksdag standing committees concerned with Bills, and peak periods are inevitable again in connection with the strictly scheduled financial year: work on the budget looms large in late Autumn and early Winter and again about midsummer when directive letters, etc., have to be prepared for issue in conjunction with appropriations. Here one may discern one of the purposes of the overhaul of departmental organization: the relief of the hard-pressed Under-Secretary's personnel in times of peak activity. The tempo on the Permanent Secretary's side of the department has tended to be less irregular. It is on this side, for example, that matters of administrative detail fell to be considered—applications for Swedish citizenship, requests for grants and loans, civil service appointment cases, etc. None of these activities is subject to such fluctuation as work on parliamentary business.

The strands of this discussion of the Chancery may now be drawn together before a look is briefly taken at procedure in departments and boards and before an attempt is made to estimate the practical significance of the decentralized nature of the administrative system. The 1965 reforms are likely to enhance the position of the Chancery as the focal point of the system by making more staff available for long-term planning and co-ordination work and by reorganizing departmental structure so as to give this function a more prominent place. The degree of political involvement that has long marked the top administrative echelons is regarded by the Swedes as helping to ensure that execution conforms to the spirit as well as to the letter of the laws. At the same time the process of circulating draft legislation, etc., on remit to the various administrative agencies concerned leaves the decision-making power firmly at the centre, and the extent to which under-secretaries in particular are used on commissions of inquiry—another reason why their task is such an arduous one—helps to ensure that the Chancery remains in ultimate control. But these last two points are best left for development in another context.[27]

Departmental business is disposed of at what is termed literally "the weekly preparation" (*veckoberedningen*) in the presence of the

[27] Chapter 5.

Minister.[28] Now that the pace is no longer so leisurely, additional meetings at set times each week are sometimes found necessary. Items of business on the parliamentary side, in particular, may require several sessions, and the Minister may be brought in on them at the early stages. The "preparation" is, of course, for formal decision by the King in Council, but the decision-taking power rests with the Minister unless the business involves other departments or is important enough to warrant cabinet consideration. Naturally he often depends heavily on the recommendations made to him. Business is introduced by the civil servant concerned with the preparation of it, i.e. always now by the appropriate *huvudman*, sometimes after consultation with the relevant board. Many lesser questions are settled by delegation in accordance with convention.

The relevant Minister without Portfolio may be consulted by telephone or may have minuted his opinion on the appropriate documents. Questions involving other departments—and notably the Finance Department—are prepared jointly with them. It should be added that the senior officials are, as one would expect, kept posted of incoming business by the Registry and supervise the more important items themselves. Since the departments are small, procedures are relatively flexible and informal. Expert civil service advisers may also be brought in to help with the preparation of particular questions (they are seconded to the department for the purpose from another sector of the administration—it may be, from a board).

Some General Observations on the Decentralized Sector

A look may now be taken at administrative organization and procedure in the decentralized boards. The subject is a vast and untidy one, since the variety of forms is such that to virtually every rule there are exceptions. Some general principles can, however, be discerned.

The directors-general in charge of boards are administrators

[28] See Heckscher, *op. cit.*, pp. 213–14, and Nordenstam, *op. cit.*, pp. 248–9, for accounts of these meetings.

rather than specialists even though, as in the case of many scientific and technical boards, they may be scientists or technologists by training.[29] The nearer one gets to the top, the more is a general administrative talent required; the further down the hierarchy one goes, the greater the degree of specialization. The exact degree of subdivision into small specialist units naturally depends on the size of the agency, but the commonest type of structure is that in which the units immediately below the level of the governing board[30] are called bureaux and are themselves subdivided into sections. In the largest agencies the bureaux are grouped into divisions, which then form the most important sub-unit.

The traditional type of governing board is that composed of the Director-General together with the heads of divisions or bureaux immediately below him. The commonest procedure for decision-taking in this type of board, so far as the more important questions coming up at the top level are concerned, is for the Director-General to decide matters on his own responsibility after obligatory consultation with the other members of the board—what the Swedes call the "semi-collegial" type of decision-taking. Dissentients are required to minute their disagreement under this procedure. Many of the less important questions coming up at top level are, however, decided by the Director-General alone and without consultation. Very often the Director-General has the assistance of a deputy who deputizes for him as the need arises; and an arrangement is commonly reached (or stipulated by the relevant instruction) whereby business is divided up between the two, each official settling items coming up from specified divisions or bureaux. Alongside these two kinds of decision-taking procedure there is a third, the fully collegial, which is the most time-hallowed of the three in the Swedish administrative system. This implies, at least in its most traditional form, a collective decision and, in case of disagreement, a vote by the entire board according to a set ritual: the civil servant introducing the business votes first, then voting proceeds in upward order of

[29] Civil service recruitment and training is discussed further in Chapter 4.

[30] I.e. the "board" in the strict or narrow sense. The word is also used to denote the agency at large.

seniority—and a casting vote by the chairman (i.e. the Director-General) settles the issue in the event of a tie. This procedure is derived from the courts and is one of many signs of the extent to which legal traditions have penetrated the public service in Sweden. In many boards its use is confined to the occasional (very rare) serious disciplinary case, in which the board is in any event acting like a court.

Of recent years a marked tendency has set in to reconstitute a number of boards by removing the divisional and bureau heads from them and bringing in laymen instead (with the Director-General remaining as chairman). The Hydroelectric board provided an early precedent for this: from the time of its foundation in 1908 it consisted of the Director-General plus four part-time directors representative of industrial, commercial, and technical experience. The primary purpose here was, of course, to ensure that good business practice was followed in board operations. In 1962 the Government reconstituted the boards of all the trading agencies along these lines. Some boards in the non-trading area have been similarly remodelled (e.g. the Social Welfare Board) and new ones have been created with the same general character, such as the National Traffic Safety Board (*Statens Trafikverk*). Quite often the laymen—who are, of course, always appointed by the Government—are specifically drawn from (and often nominated by) the larger and more influential organizations in Swedish society in accordance with directions contained in the instruction for the board in question. The object in such cases is partly to be able to decentralize business so that those who are most affected by a decision are associated more closely in the making of it, and partly—by the same token—to try to ensure that decisions once taken shall be smoothly executed and readily obeyed. A case in point is the Labour Market Board, where only a small minority of the members are civil servants (they include, however, the Director-General and his deputy) and where most of the remainder are required to be representative of particular organizations: two, for example, come from the Swedish Employers' Federation, two from the TUC, one from the Swedish Confederation of Professional Associations, and one from the

Association of Salaried Employees[31]—while, more generally, women and the agricultural interest are also to have representation. The net effect of these provisions is to cause employee and worker organizations' representatives to outnumber the employers on the board. Agreed solutions are, however, sought, and there is no sharp regular cleavage along rigid lines. The lay members are appointed for 3-year terms. The bureau chiefs of the Labour Market Board are not members of the Board, but they are expected to sit in on its deliberations and to record any disagreement they may feel with its decisions. This arrangement is, of course, designed to bring the views of the professional administrators to government notice. It has parallels in other boards.[32]

Forms of lay membership vary considerably. The Housing Board, for example, consists of a Director-General, his deputy, and five lay members who should *not* represent particular organizations: it is responsible for supervising loans granted for housing purposes within a framework set by the Government. Tribunals, on the other hand, which deal with industrial and certain welfare questions and which legally are equivalent to boards, are carefully composed to allow of equal representation for both sides of industry—the chairman being naturally impartial. Again, MPs are commonly to be found as board members, but more usually as laymen than because of their party allegiance. Cases such as the new Police Board, where all the major parties are represented, are unusual.

In general, the more important questions are reserved for collective decision in lay boards and the old legalistic procedures for "collegial" decision-making are not followed in them. A considerable volume of business has, in the nature of the case, to be settled by the Director-General acting alone.

Two final points should be made in connection with the com-

[31] The Association of Salaried Employees (TCO) represents state, local authority, and private enterprise employees alike.

[32] I am much indebted to J.-Å. Wickléus for kind permission for the use of some material here from his unpublished essay, "Föredragnings- och besluts-former inom arbetsmarknadsstyrelsens styrelse", Stockholm University, Political Science Department, Spring term, 1963.

position of boards. Firstly, there is a growing tendency for an official from one administrative unit to be allocated a place on a board in a similar field. Sometimes this takes the form of a Chancery civil servant being made a board member (Finance Department—State Collective Bargaining Board), and an official from one board may be given a seat on another (Labour Market Board—School Board). Secondly, the professional administrators are generally likely to retain a considerable influence even on boards with a lay majority.[33]

The boards themselves, then, may be either lay or professional in composition, though in almost every case they will have a professional head: their staffs are civil servants. It is, of course, here in the lower echelons that the vast majority of the decisions taken in the name of the board are reached—by bureau heads, section chiefs, etc. The preparation of business for decision often involves the holding of committee meetings, conferences with other bureaux affected, fact-finding journeys, etc.—normal procedures in most administrative systems. But the traditional pattern in Sweden is to associate two officials in the decision-taking process. Strictly speaking it is only one, the superior, who decides; the other prepares the material for decision by doing the necessary research, checking the precedents and the existing state of the law on the subject, for example, and consulting any relevant authorities. The results of this activity are then presented orally, usually together with a positive proposal as to the form the decision should take. If the man introducing the business disagrees with the way in which his superior settles it, he is supposed to record his dissent in the minutes. However, as one commentator puts it:

> It has been held that it is too much to ask a lower official, who is dependent on the goodwill of his chief for promotion, to show his dif-

---

[33] On boards, see L. Foyer, Uppgifter och organisation, in Andrén and others (ed.), *Svensk statsförvaltning i omdaning*, pp. 13–49. See also L. Foyer, *Former för kontakt och samverkan mellan staten och organisationera*, Stockholm 1961 (reprint from SOU, 1961: 21), chapter 3; Heckscher, *op. cit., passim*; D. V. Verney, *op. cit., passim*; Tore Petrén, *Domstolar, departement och ämbetsverk*, Rabén och Sjögren, Ystad, 1962.

> ference of opinion in so demonstrative a manner as by making an entry in the minutes. The circumstances that this happens extremely seldom in practice bears witness to the fact that the system does not work in the way intended.[34]

Routine matters are usually settled by sending in the relevant papers to the appropriate superior together with a written proposal for decision, or else (increasingly) by allowing one and the same official to prepare and decide them.

Practice in respect of the registration of business and minute-keeping varies considerably from board to board. Thus registers may be kept centrally for the whole agency or separately by sub-units within it—or both. It may be mentioned that when individual interests suffer because of defective registration or filing techniques the Ombudsman is apt to intervene. On some occasions, defective registration results in a bypassing of the rule that official documents shall be public; on others, confusion in the files may result in delays in handling of business. The 1965 report of the Ombudsman for Civil Affairs records, for example, that it was not possible to obtain from the files of a particular Provincial Housing Board any clear picture of the current situation in respect of applications for housing loans, with consequent delays in the settlement of business.[35]

No account of the Swedish administrative system would be complete without a mention of the parliamentary sector and of the state trading companies. The parliamentary sector includes—apart from the offices of the Ombudsman, the Swedish Office of the Nordic Council, and the Riksdag Library—two agencies which have long been under Riksdag control, namely the Bank of Sweden and the National Debt Office. The Bank of Sweden, which has the usual central banking functions of controlling the issue of paper-money, conducting open-market operations, and generally supervising credit policy on the home front as well as administering foreign currency reserves, originated as a private bank in 1957 and was taken over by Parliament in 1668. It is administered by a board of seven, six of

[34] B. Wennergren, *op. cit.*, pp. 59–60.
[35] JO report, 1965, pp. 431–42.

whom are MPs chosen roughly according to the PR principle by a special Riksdag electoral college. The board serves for a renewable 3-year term, one-third retiring annually. The seventh member, who is the chairman, is appointed by the Government for 3 years at a time. This board elects the Governor of the Bank from among its own number. It supervises a smaller and more professional body which is charged with the immediate control of operations. Foreign reserves are administered by a special panel, four of whose members are government-appointed and three of whom are selected by the board of the Bank.

The National Debt Office (*Riksgäldskontoret*) dates from 1789,[36] when the Riksdag took over the debts incurred by King Gustav III as a result of war with Russia and Denmark: the King was not to raise any loans in future without parliamentary approval. The board is elected in the same way and according to the same principles as the board of the Bank, except that the chairman in this case is not government-appointed but is separately elected by the same Riksdag electoral college. The immediate administration is carried out by bureaux under the general supervision of the board. The traditional duty of the office is, as the name implies, the administration of the national debt; its chief task today to raise loans to finance the capital budget as well as for certain other purposes.[37]

The general policy of both the Bank and the National Debt Office is determined by the economic policy of the Government. Thus the main guidelines for the activity of the Bank are laid down by law, while the framework for the activity of the National Debt Office is largely fixed by the budget. These circumstances have prompted a legal observer to remark:

> The "parliamentary boards" are traditionally usually distinguished from the state administration proper, since they do not come under the government, but with present-day conceptions of government there can

---

[36] A similar agency had, however, administered the National Debt on behalf of the Riksdag between 1719 and 1765.

[37] N. Andrén, *Modern Swedish Government*, pp. 135–6, gives further details of these loans.

> be no doubt but that they are organs of the state: the dualistic way of looking at government in which they grew up is outdated.[38]

Nevertheless, the article of the Instrument of Government which forbids the King (or Government) to issue direct orders to the boards of the Bank and the Debt Office[39] is not a dead letter, and the Bank has an independent power to vary the interest rates on its credits, while the National Debt Office can use its own initiative to borrow moneys when necessary to meet charges upon it.[40] The boards of both agencies, finally, send their reports and requests to the Riksdag via the Committee on Banking (one of the standing committees), and this committee has the right to give them directives within the framework of parliamentary regulations (no very extensive power in practice).

On the outermost fringe, so to speak, of the Swedish administrative system are the State companies, of which there are just over two dozen.[41] The companies have been created for a variety of reasons. Some, like *Nya System AB*, which has a monopoly of the sale of alcoholic beverages, was set up for a mixture of fiscal and welfare reasons (this particular company was established in 1954, but with a progenitor in 1917). Others, like the Swedish Shale Oil Co. (*Svenska Skifferolje AB*), are a byproduct of defence preparations dating from 1940 to 1941. Others mark rescuing operations in connection with private concerns—e.g. LKAB, the big iron-mining concern in the north and the oldest State company of them all (partly nationalized in 1907, fully in 1957). Others, again, represent conversions from earlier trading agencies—like *Svenska Reproduktions AB*, a printing concern (founded 1927, converted to company form 1962). The list could be extended. The share capital for these companies is raised by Parliament, which is thereby afforded the chance to lay down the principles regulating their activity. The fact that shares are

[38] N. Herlitz, *Den offentliga förvaltningens organisation* (*Föreläsningar i förvaltningsrätt*, II), Stockholm, 2nd edn., Norstedt, 1948, pp. 18–19.

[39] RF, article 111.

[40] Malmgren, *op. cit.*, p. 73.

[41] A list is given in Arne Brodd, *op. cit.*, p. 197. Verney, *op. cit.*, has a good deal of information on the subject generally.

owned by the State allows state representation, of course, at the shareholders' annual general meeting and a chance of more immediate control.[42] Agreements regulating company activity in the state interest may be entered into, and a further opportunity for supervision occurs when companies make application for loans, etc. But the employees of the companies are in no sense civil servants; the publicity of public documents rule does not apply in this sector; and the normal financial operations of the companies are purely their own concern—e.g. profits do not have to be surrendered to the Exchequer.

This discursive, but still necessarily rather summary, review of the outlines of the Swedish administrative system may be concluded by attempting an answer to the last of the three questions raised earlier in this chapter, the question of the significance under present-day circumstances of the decentralized character of the system. It would, in the first place, be artificial and unreal to describe the division of labour between the central departments and the boards just in terms of a division between the policy-making sector, on the one hand, and the sector engaged in day-to-day administration, on the other. The departments, as has been seen, do have some administrative work to perform; the boards, by virtue of their executive functions, naturally have an interest in the gestation of policy within their sphere of activity. The commission of inquiry may have come to overshadow the board at the preparatory stage of reforms, but it has to be remembered, firstly, that the original impulse towards the setting up of a commission of inquiry may come from a board (acting on the appropriate department), and secondly, that the directors-general of boards quite often serve on commissions of inquiry within the area of their expertise. Boards are, as was noted earlier, expected to keep abreast of developments in their field and to come in with proposals for change when they think this necessary. Central co-ordination by the Chancery is likely to be assisted by the

[42] The companies are attached to particular departments, and the opposition on the Standing Committee on the Constitution complained in 1961 about the practice of choosing civil servants from the relevant departments to represent the State shareholding interest in some cases (KU mem. 15, 1961).

growth in departmental planning staffs, but this has been accompanied by a growth of planning staffs in the decentralized sector, so that the interest of the boards in policy matters is likely to quicken still further. The circulation of draft proposals for reform to administrative agencies for comment has already been referred to as a device which enables the experts to give their views a public airing and the boards to bring some influence to bear at the formative stage of policy-making. The government can hence be required to clarify its attitude on doubtful or debatable technical points at an early stage. Summing up thus far, decentralization helps to ensure a thoroughness and an openness in the preparation of legislation that is bought at the cost of a certain slowness and formalism. Sometimes there is duplication in the treatment of business as between boards and departments, but this is not considered too heavy a price to pay for the compensating advantages.

Secondly, the system helps to free the central departments for their primary task of long-term planning and policy making. It allows the rapid promotion of able and energetic younger men (sometimes, as was seen, politically oriented) to positions of responsibility in the Chancery, and it enables them to be moved out at a later stage to positions of responsibility in the predominantly executive decentralized sector.

Thirdly, decentralization has helped to block the emergence of a doctrine of ministerial responsibility as understood in Britain. This in turn, as was mentioned in the last chapter, has had consequences for the proceedings in the Riksdag and, more importantly, helps to reinforce the principle of the individual responsibility of the civil servant for his actions. Both these points are examined further at a later stage.

Fourthly, decentralization has not invariably meant that administrative agencies have enjoyed a higher degree of freedom from central control than agencies carrying out similar functions in Britain. A comparison of the position of the Swedish trading agencies with the nationalized industries in Britain would be much to the point in this context. There has, in fact, been steady pressure from nationalized industries in Sweden for increased autonomy within the past decade or so. This pressure has, as seen, met with some success, and it may be noted that the report of an inquiry on the subject late in 1968 has recommended further steps in the same direction.

Fifthly, the structure of the system has probably made it easier to allow play to the pluralism of Swedish society by associating the representatives of interested groups and organizations directly with the administrative process. The growth of lay membership on the boards is an important point in this connection. At the same time, there has not been the same incentive as in Britain for the establishment of a great number of advisory committees working in close contact with the central departments.

CHAPTER 4

The Civil Service

THERE are rather more than half a million people in the service of public authorities in Sweden, roughly a sixth of the total working population.[1] This includes those employed in the local government sector. The number of people in state service proper comes to slightly under a third of a million, approximately a tenth of the total working population. Subtracting manual workers in state employment, we are left with a total of a quarter of a million civil servants. Few of these, as has been seen, work directly in the central departments: the great majority work in the trading agencies and defence administration and the central boards, many of these latter operating outside Stockholm at regional or even, in some cases, at local level. It will be apparent that many of those who work in the decentralized administrative agencies are engaged in operations which in Britain would be the direct responsibility of a ministry—running overseas aid programmes, labour exchanges, public works and buildings, etc. Others, again, are doing work of a kind that would fall to the employees of public corporations in Britain—those employed by Swedish Railways, for example, or in the electricity supply industry (which is not, however, a state monopoly in Sweden). Others, notably the doctors and nurses in the state sector, would be in the NHS, or else, like certain categories of teacher, would be local government employees—though in both the health and education fields the state sector in Sweden is overshadowed by the local government sector if the criterion is the number of per-

[1] Cf., for example Erik Höök, *Den offentliga sektorns expansion*, Almqvist and Wiksell, Uppsala, 1962, pp. 42–43, and Hans Garke, Den statliga tjänstemannakårens omfattning och struktur, in Andrén *et al.*, *op. cit.*, pp. 163–9.

sonnel employed. Others, finally, like university staffs or river pilots, would not be reckoned part of the public service at all.

The decentralization of the Swedish administrative system naturally has repercussions on the organization and structure of the civil service. Thus there is no body corresponding to the Civil Service Commission with a responsibility for the centralized recruitment of large numbers of civil servants. Civil servants in the higher echelons are certainly appointed centrally by the Government, but in the majority of cases within this category the nomination of candidates is made by the agencies with which the recruits are to serve. Recruitment in general remains firmly in the hands of the separate authorities.

The same decentralized pattern has, with some significant exceptions, long obtained in matters of training. Many administrative agencies—notably the great trading agencies—virtually have their own career structures and their own often lengthy and extensive training programmes. Many civil servants, again, in the lower and middle ranks of the service, have had no training courses of any kind: their entrance qualifications and the process of learning on the job have been considered adequate for service requirements. Of recent years greater attention has been paid centrally to the question of training, and the Department of Civil Service Affairs (which is in general but a shadow of its former self as the result of the shedding of some of its most important functions to decentralized agencies) has been responsible for promoting experimental work in this field. A departmental inquiry into staff training was set up in 1961, and a staff training unit (created that same year) has been operating a number of short courses for, for example, new recruits on the first rung of what might be called the higher civil service ladder (the recruits come from both departments and boards) and also for higher civil servants comparatively new to senior posts. Training in standard administrative procedures and practices bulks large in the course for new recruits, while for senior men, e.g. management and economic, questions are staple elements of the tuition provided. The scale of these operations is modest, however: they are probably best regarded as pilot schemes. A new phase seems likely to be heralded by the creation, in July 1967, of a centralized Staff Training Commission.

In certain areas—health, schools, and much of the social welfare front—state and local government administration are closely interwoven, and the boundaries between them are more blurred in some respects than is the case in Britain. Space does not allow a closer exploration of this theme, which is in any case tangential to the present survey; but it is worth remarking that civil servants in these sectors may occasionally be required to serve with local authorities in the interests of flexible and efficient administration—without loss of pay or privileges. The state sector, in short, is not entirely a rigidly self-contained system. Terms of appointment, again, vary considerably and permit both of direct recruitment to responsible posts from outside the service and also theoretically of considerable organizational flexibility. But this topic will be looked at more closely later.

What is the justification, it may be asked, for regarding the staffs of this galaxy of independent agencies as members of a civil service properly so called? The Swedes themselves define a civil servant differently for different purposes.[2] Without delving into the intricacies of Swedish administrative law (a discipline which still accounts for a high percentage of the books on Swedish government, although the situation is fast changing), unity is imposed on the system in part by means of an elaborate standardized structure of pay scales which are common to departments and boards. Terms of appointment, though varied, fall into a number of legally prescribed categories. Conditions of service follow distinctly uniform patterns. Standardized disciplinary rules apply.[3] One can discern the existence of a lower, middle, and higher career for some (by no means all) civil servants engaged in general administration: the regularities are not as clear-cut as in the case of the Treasury classes in Britain (classes now, of course, scheduled for abolition.) Much of the uniformity in conditions of service, etc., is due to the efforts of the four

[2] See proposition, 1965: 60, pp. 54 et seq. Also Ingmar Lidbeck, Begreppen tjänsteman och statstjänsteman, in Andrén *et al.*, *op. cit.*, pp. 157–62.

[3] The civil servant's liability for his actions is discussed in Chapter 6.

main unions to which civil servants belong, namely (1) the Swedish Confederation of Professional Associations (SACO), which is what its name implies and whose membership stretches out beyond the public sector to include graduates in professional work in industry, etc.; (2) the National Federation of Civil Servants (SR), the small but influential union for the higher ranks of the service; (3) the Central Organization of Salaried Employees (TCO), which might fairly be described as the national white-collar workers' union, so that its membership, like that of SACO, extends beyond the public sector; and (4) the Civil Service Association (*Statstjänarkartellen*), a union for those in the lower echelons, affiliated to the Swedish TUC.

It was shown in the previous chapter that open political commitment is no bar to holding posts in the Swedish administrative system, notably at the under-secretaryship level in the Chancery, but not by any means exclusively there. The civil service in general may fairly be described as a non-political career service, but it should be said at this point that the conventions regulating the political activities of civil servants are much less restrictive than is the case in Britain. It is possible for even a highly placed regular civil servant, for example, to stand for the Riksdag and, if successful, to retain his place in the service. The possibility is not exploited much under modern conditions: only a handful of Riksdagsmen can be said to hold high administrative office. The exact number is not easy to determine because of classification difficulties, but three or four cases could be discerned in both Houses combined at the beginning of 1965, including a bureau chief from the Housing Board who sat in the Upper House in the Social Democratic interest, and another from the Prisons Board sitting in the Lower House as a Liberal. There is always a fair sprinkling of MPs, however, from other areas of the public service—in 1965, for example, a Crown forester, labour exchange men, a factory inspector, a surveyor, and, of course, teachers, army officers, and Lutheran clergy.

Historical reasons go far towards explaining the phenomenon of the civil service MP in Sweden. The central administration was virtually an aristocratic preserve from its earliest days until quite late in the eighteenth century, and the aristocracy continued to be a powerful element in it throughout the nineteenth century also. State officials were consequently to be found in strength in the Estate of the Nobility until the abolition of the unreformed Parliament in 1866. Thereafter the tradition carried over into the new legislature, so that for a long time after 1866 civil servants—fewer and fewer of them belonging to the ranks of the nobility[4]—formed a numerous and influential bloc of MPs, especially in the Upper House. They tended throughout the nineteenth century to follow the line of the government of the day, governments at this period being strongly bureaucratic in character themselves. This brought them into ill repute with early Liberal and Agrarian party groups, and the agitation for a widening of the suffrage was designed in part to bring about a reduction of bureaucratic power.[5] The numbers of civil service MPs have dwindled steadily this century, the growth of the party system and the increasing burden of official work making it more and more difficult for those in the more responsible positions to combine the two activities satisfactorily. Nevertheless, civil servants at whatever level are considered to be as entitled as those in any profession to offer themselves for election to the Riksdag, and if successful they may be granted leave of absence from their official work or they may, if circumstances allow, combine the two activities. [This, incidentally, provided another justification for the old constitutional ban on the parliamentary discussion of specific administrative measures: a high-ranking civil servant could find the ladder of degree being shaken by one of his subordinates who had managed to get himself elected to the Riksdag.] At all events the convention is now firmly established that any political differences with the government of the day shall not be carried over into the job, where loyal service is required irrespective of political affiliation.

A more significant feature of the Swedish civil service is the part

[4] The last person to be ennobled in Sweden was the explorer Sven Hedin, in 1902.

[5] Per Hultqvist, Riksdagsopinionen mot ämbetsmannaintressena. Från representationsreformen till 1880—talets början, *Acta Universitatis Gotoburgensis*, 1954: 5 (Gothenburg), is a scholarly study of this period.

played in it by those with a legal training. An official survey carried out in 1950 into the educational background of some 16,000 civil servants in responsible positions in departments and boards revealed that some 30 per cent of those with higher educational qualifications (7612 of the total number surveyed had such qualifications) had taken the *juris kandidat*, the standard law degree.[6] This was by far the largest single category of those having higher educational qualifications outside the scientific and technological field, outnumbering those with arts degrees by roughly 3 to 1 in this survey. Social scientists with specialist qualifications formed only a sprinkling of the total, and even within the sector of the administration concerned with economic affairs persons with an economics degree (the *civilekonom*) were at that time outnumbered roughly 5 to 2 by the lawyers. The preponderance of lawyers was particularly noticeable in the departments of State and in the older and more traditional parts of the administration—77 per cent, for instance, of those with higher educational qualifications in the Chancery had taken the basic law degree. More recently there has been a marked shift in the overall balance in favour of arts graduates (most of whom in fact have some general social science qualifications, the university faculties being then undifferentiated), but legally qualified people still predominate at the upper levels of the hierarchy.[7] Thus a check on the classifications given for the higher civil servants in the Chancery in the 1965 *State Calendar* showed that, if experts imported into the departments on *ad hoc* duties are left out of account, approximately 61 per cent of those with a higher educational qualification could be reckoned as lawyers by training, and the total rises to approximately 66 per cent if those with a combination of legal and other degrees are taken into consideration.

The powerful influence of lawyers in the Swedish Administration can be traced historically to the fact that the administrative and

[6] A general survey of the educational background of civil servants at that time is given in SOU, 1953: 15 and 16, *Juridisk och samhällsvetenstapliga utbildning*. Figures in text from SOU, 1953: 16, pp. 35 et seq.

[7] A table based on October 1963 figures is given in Hans Garke, *op. cit.*, p. 169.

judicial functions were early regarded as closely akin: in both cases the primary duty was the application of the law. More particularly, the entire administrative system has long been subject to close regulation by law. Administrative agencies were, moreover, given judicial functions from the very start of a strong centralized administration, and a pattern of administrative appeals (*besvär*) developed early. In these circumstances a marked *rechtstaat* tradition soon began to appear. Civil servants came to be expected to act independently of their superiors in the determination of issues affecting the rights of individuals. The procedures of public authorities became pervaded by a formalism which was considered to be both a symbol of and a safeguard for the dispensing of even-handed justice from one case to the next. These traditional attitudes have become harder to maintain as the State has expanded its activities rapidly in the social and economic field. The demand for other, often newer, varieties of expertise has grown apace, and inevitably there has been a corresponding decline in the relative importance of the lawyer within the public service. The change has duly been noted and lamented by commentators of the traditional school. Thus, in the words of one distinguished legal expert: "The chances . . . of the administration causing severe economic damage to private persons have . . . greatly multiplied, at the same time that a declining quality among authorities and public servants has made improper measures a more and more common phenomenon with more and more serious consequences."[8] This assessment may be taken in part as the reflection of a conservatism which has at times found expression in milder forms in the more traditional sectors of the administration itself, e.g. when proposals for reconstructing degree courses to meet the changing needs of the public service have come up for review.

Persons with a legal training are likely to continue to play an important part in the Swedish civil service for a long time to come. Decentralization is linked with the regulation of administrative activity by formal rules, and the individual responsibility of civil servants reinforces the importance of their knowing the legal ropes. Administrative coherence and consistency owe much to the elaborate

[8] H. G. F. Sundberg, *Allmän förvaltningsrätt*, Gleerup, Lund, 1962, p. 399.

system of administrative appeals. Administrative and judicial functions continue to be closely combined in some sectors of the system: a notable (if somewhat extreme) instance is the Exchequer Board, which handles questions affecting land titles, water rights, the administration of Church lands, and the territorial boundaries of ecclesiastical and local government authorities (it also looks after the Swedish Crown jewels). Not surprisingly, therefore, it is an agency dominated by lawyers. The changed climate of opinion in which the lawyers operate can be clearly illustrated in this field: the administration of the local government boundary sector has been less concerned of late with the adjudication of local disputes than with arrangements in connection with the enactment of two drastic instalments of local government reform inside the space of two decades.

Circulation of personnel from the courts to the administration and back again occurs in a few cases, as was mentioned in the last chapter,[9] at the director-generalship level of boards. It is, however, by no means confined to that. Judges from the appeal courts (*hovrättsråd*), and other legal officials from these courts, can and sometimes do work for a spell in the legal sections of the Chancery in the course of their career. They may, again, do service as secretaries to commissions of inquiry. The instructions of some boards, even in the trading agency sector, occasionally specify that certain posts shall be filled by persons with legal qualifications, and experience of work in the lower courts (district courts or *ting*) may be accounted a merit in this connection. Preference, again, may be given in practice to those with court experience when filling *amanuens* positions in certain boards, these positions being virtually the first step on the ladder of a higher career: the preference may be given in practice without being formally prescribed. Over much of the field, though, preference is nowadays given to persons with research degrees in arts or social sciences in areas likely to be of use to the agency concerned.

It should perhaps be mentioned at this point that university law courses in Sweden are tailored to some extent to meet the needs of the state service—a circumstance which is relevant when considering

[9] pp. 77–78.

the question of post-entry training. Thus provision was made for a 5-month basic course in economics as part of the 4½-year first law degree course as a result of a reform carried out in the late 1950's:[10] the emphasis in this economics course was designed to be on branches of the subject likely to be of value to an administrator—e.g. elementary statistics, trade cycle theory, costing techniques, etc. (with an extra 2–3 months for those seeking higher qualifications). The regular law course contains optional orientation courses in social science subjects such as sociology and political science—or again, a would-be lawyer could decide to specialize to a greater extent in the social sciences and opt for a combined course in which criminal law and a part of civil law drops out of the syllabus, allowing time for statistics, political science, and economics together with some more advanced work in one of these latter disciplines. A combined course of this kind is obviously useful for the law student with his sights on an administrative career.

Arts graduates, frequently including those with some grounding in social science, have, as was mentioned earlier, been increasing steadily in numbers in the civil service and are nearing parity with the lawyers at the topmost levels. Persons with specialized degrees in political science, economics, and sociology have been numbered in hundreds rather than thousands, but their importance is rapidly increasing. Arrangements in force since 1947 have enabled accelerated promotion to be given within limits to satisfactory recruits to the higher career in departments, boards, and provincial governments provided that they have higher educational qualifications of particular value to the agency concerned.

Persons with scientific or technical degrees form another major bloc of higher civil servants in Sweden. They were, in fact, the most numerous single category of those with higher educational qualifications covered by the 1950 survey (39 per cent of the total)[11] and they are almost as plentiful as lawyers in the more highly paid positions within the state service—although this applies to the boards, not to the departments, where they are rare. Engineers are the largest

[10] Proposition, 1957: 86.

[11] SOU, 1953: 16, p. 36.

single group amongst them. Technologists and scientists are not organized into one class common to all administrative agencies, but they are anything but a depressed group within the state service. Sweden is a country with a number of technical high schools comparable in status to universities and the social status of technologists, scientists, etc., has long been high. More to the point in the present context, there is no reluctance to fill the top administrative posts of scientific and technical agencies with scientific and technical men. Again, it is quite a common practice for people without advanced technical or scientific qualifications to be taken on by, for example, the Telecommunications Board or the Railways Board, then to acquire additional qualifications by means of courses run by the boards themselves and to rise by their own efforts through the hierarchy. Relatively humble recruits can, as was mentioned earlier, forge a satisfactory career for themselves within the one agency: it is in general easier to rise higher from small beginnings in this sphere than in the older and more traditional sectors of the administrative system. Salaries, however, tend to be higher in the private sector, and it has already been seen that the rigid pay structure of the public service tends to put difficulties in the way of rewarding men of particular merit. To some extent employment on a contractual basis is used to get round this difficulty.

Some of the most important general rules concerning civil service appointments, security of tenure, etc., were for long enshrined in the basic laws and needed the full process of constitutional amendment to be brought into play before they could be changed. Thus it was laid down in the 1809 Instrument of Government, for example, that no civil servant except for the holder of a fiduciary post could be removed from his job unless after trial and conviction in a court of law—and neither could he be transferred to another post unless at his own request.[12] In other words, a man was considered to have a right to his post once he had acquired it, so that older civil servants used to have to be bought out of office by new entrants or else simply stay on until they died (a practice not, of course, peculiar to Sweden). The fiduciary posts—those which were to be held during

[12] RF, para. 36.

the King's pleasure—were enumerated in the constitution[13] and included provincial governorships, diplomatic appointments, and the headships of certain administrative boards.

The regulation of civil service terms of appointment in this way by constitutional prescription reflected, of course, the degree of influence enjoyed by civil servants in the Riksdag and the old tradition of civil service independence of the Crown so far as the enjoyment of office was concerned (the irremovability clause, for example, can be traced back to 1611). Not until 1965 were most of the basic rules affecting tenure taken out of the Instrument of Government and incorporated into ordinary law. They had inevitably become a poor guide to practice long before that, and a variety of rather casuistical expedients had been resorted to in order to evade the letter of the law and to facilitate reorganizations in the service.

A look may now be taken at the Civil Service Act of 1965.[14] It was notable in part for first legalizing civil service strikes and lockouts by the state. Strike action is only permissible within clearly defined limits. Thus only strikes which are officially approved by the unions are in order: wildcat and unofficial strikes incur liability for prosecution or disciplinary action or, in certain circumstances, for damages. Sympathetic strikes cannot be undertaken in the state sector in connection with labour disputes outside that sector. Only matters coming within the sphere allowed for collective bargaining can be made the basis for strike action. Such matters include, first and foremost, salaries; secondly, pension rights; and, thirdly, such conditions of service questions as hours of work, holiday rights, etc. As far as pay is concerned, the expectation plainly is that terms will be agreed collectively for periods of 2 years or so at a time (in parallel with precedent and with general industrial practice). Conflict over these negotiable matters is thus likeliest to break out in the event of a deadlock over a proposed new agreement. Civil servants cannot, of course, be subject to disciplinary action or other penalty for taking strike action under such circumstances. Both they and their unions are liable for damages should they take part in union-sponsored

[13] RF, para. 35.

[14] The relevant proposition is 1965: 60.

strikes in connection with prohibited subjects. Among these prohibited subjects may be mentioned establishment questions in a broad sense—the creation of new posts and the abolition of old ones, the allocation of work within an administrative agency, etc. These are considered to be organizational matters properly within the jurisdiction of the authority concerned.[15] Individual appointments and dismissals, again, are not subject to collective bargaining or strike action: disputes in connection with them are to continue to be settled through the traditional process of the administrative appeal. Go-slows, overtime bans, etc., are proscribed: aggrieved civil servants may only resort to strike action. Questions of liability for damages, and also questions concerning the interpretation of collective agreements already negotiated, are settled by a tribunal specializing in industrial disputes—the Labour Court. In disputes threatening a breakdown of essential services, a special conciliation procedure was prescribed in accordance with an agreement entered into between the State, on the one hand, and the civil service unions on the other. In the event of a breakdown in relations after this conciliation procedure had been exhausted, industrial action can still be taken—but the Government retains the right to take special measures to maintain key services and supplies.

The freedom to strike conferred on the Swedish civil servant by the 1965 Act received considerable publicity abroad when, in October 1966, salary negotiations for teachers broke down between the Swedish Confederation of Professional Associations, on the one hand, and the State Collective Bargaining Board,[16] on the other: the Board resorted to a lockout and the union called its civil service members out on strike. This dispute was bitter though short-lived. There had been earlier conflicts in the public sector (e.g. over nurses' pay in 1951) in the years since 1937, when an Order-in-Council made it the duty of administrative authorities to consult with civil

[15] Consultation of civil service unions by administrative agencies in connection with rationalization schemes, etc., is, of course, perfectly permissible.

[16] *Statens avtalsverk*—a new agency which has taken over duties previously exercised by the Department of Civil Service Affairs in the collective bargaining field.

service organizations before reaching decisions on salary questions, etc. But in these cases only clumsy weapons had been available on either side—threats of mass resignations, for example, or of the withholding by the State of negotiated pay rises.

The 1965 Act, apart from introducing the right to strike, also codified and modernized some of the basic rules governing civil service terms of appointment, discipline, conditions of service, etc. Disciplinary matters are looked at in Chapter 6: terms of appointment are a complex subject and are best dealt with briefly within a wider frame of reference.

The Government, as has been seen, has full discretion in the making of appointments to posts at the topmost level of the hierarchy—director-generalships, under-secretaries, etc. It can, for example, choose between promoting a man from the agency concerned and bringing in one from elsewhere in the administration, or, if it wishes to do so, it may import someone from outside the civil service altogether. The relevant minister is often influential in making an initial recommendation.

Below this level, the rule is that the Government formally appoints to all the posts in the higher pay brackets. The extent of government appointment varies from one sector of the administration to another, being at a maximum in the Chancery and a minimum in the trading agencies. Appointments are usually made automatically on the recommendation of the appropriate director-general or minister. In some cases, however, appointment is made from a short-list of three candidates ranged in order of recommendation by the authority concerned: in these instances clearly the Government enjoys a greater discretion. It is also relevant to mention in this connection the task which falls to the Government of settling appeals in appointment cases over a wide range of posts lower down the pay scales. But, when all these facts have been taken into account, it remains true that the great majority of civil service vacancies are filled on a decentralized basis by the agencies themselves.

The 1965 Act follows earlier prescriptions in laying down the general rule that vacancies in posts not subject to government appointment shall be advertised so that consideration can be given to all who apply within the prescribed period. The advertisement requirement does not usually involve as much publicity as might at first appear: over much of the field it is enough for a notice to be inserted in the civil service gazette (*Post- och Inrikestidningar*), so that the competition is effectively made internal to the service. In some cases, however, it will be desired to cast the net wider and to advertise more generally, e.g. when persons with professional qualifications are required. One byproduct of the advertisement procedure, it may be noted, is that, wherever it applies, civil servants seeking promotion are required to put in for the post they desire in formal competition with all comers. Again, it is a common practice in the Swedish civil service to advertise posts on a *locum* basis when the usual incumbent is expected to be away on other official duty—it may be as secretary to a commission of inquiry or on secondment to another agency. An advertisement is usually resorted to whenever the holder of the post is away for a fairly long period of time, and the rate for the job is usually paid when the absence is expected to exceed 6 months. For lesser periods—e.g. when an official is away on holiday—a subordinate may be asked to deputize and the salary arrangements are variable.

The entrance requirements for particular posts are sometimes prescribed centrally—thus the instructions for boards may specify what is needed before persons can be considered for certain senior positions such as heads of bureaux (e.g. a law degree with or without practical experience in the courts, an engineering degree, etc). On the whole, however, it is the agencies concerned which lay down the rules. The basic principles governing the making of a choice from suitably qualified candidates continue to be a matter for regulation by the Constitution:[17] the preference is to be given solely on the grounds of "merit and ability". "Merit" in this context means seniority of service—a criterion which, in the Swedish as in many other administrative systems, appears as a general rule to weigh more heavily at the lower levels of the hierarchy.

Competitive examination, though in use in a few sectors of the

[17] RF, para. 28.

administration, is much less in favour than is the case in Britain as a method of sorting out applicants for jobs. A great many posts in the boards, and especially in the trading agencies, require specialized technical or scientific knowledge and are consequently best filled by reference to professional qualifications rather than by examination. Quite apart from this factor, however, there is often something of a flavour of judicial process about the manner of making an appointment. The criterion of "ability" laid down in the basic laws is wide enough to permit account to be taken of personal qualities. In practice, however, great weight is often attached to the written documents (including superiors' reports) accompanying applications, and this has an obvious connection with the right of appeal possessed by unsuccessful candidates. An appeal must be lodged within a specified period (3 weeks) and appellants have access to the papers in the case under the terms of the law governing the publicity of official documents. If divergent opinions are recorded, an unsuccessful candidate may find himself able to secure a reversal of the original decision the more readily.[18] There can, of course, be no appeal against government appointments to the topmost posts, but an appeal may lie against government appointments at a lower level—technically it is an appeal against the recommendation of the nominating board.

The distinction that was mentioned earlier between an upper, middle, and lower career for numbers of civil servants engaged on general administration, is not an official one but was first made by Heckscher in his pioneering work on the Swedish state service.[19] The crux of the distinction was the widespread insistence—in fact if not always in form—on a higher educational qualification of some kind before taking on new recruits at the first stage of the ladder of the higher career in the Chancery and in certain central boards. The result of this requirement was to create a virtually unbridgeable gulf between the clerical and auxiliary staffs, on the one hand, and the upper echelons, on the other. These difficulties, as has been seen, did not apply to anything like the same extent in the case of the trading agencies. The earlier sharpness of the division elsewhere has

[18] See Chapter 7, p. 155.

[19] G. Heckscher, *op. cit.*, pp. 320–4.

been softened to some extent by the spread of an intermediate class of posts from provincial governments and trading agencies to other central boards: these positions are filled partly by the promotion of able men from below, partly by the recruitment of persons with the matriculation qualification (*studentexamen*) from outside the service, and they afford slightly improved prospects of further promotion. In 1960, too, budgetary provision was made for more posts in the Chancery open to people without advanced academic attainments.

It is not surprising, in view of the educational barrier, to find that the higher-ranking posts in the Chancery and in many central boards have long been dominated by people of upper middle-class origins, coming especially from families with a professional background. It remains to be seen what impact will be made on this situation by the educational reforms which were inaugurated in 1962 and which have established the comprehensive school as the norm. Certainly only a very small percentage of the higher positions in the public service have hitherto been filled by people drawn from a working-class family background—although there are considerable variations in this respect between different sectors of the system, and (as might be anticipated) the percentage of persons of working-class origin in the upper echelons of the trading agencies is about twice the general average.[20] It is perhaps also worth a mention that the foreign affairs sector of the administration (like the armed services) still proves attractive to the sparse ranks of the aristocracy: the *1965 State Calendar*, for example, showed four barons and three counts out of just over a hundred higher officials in the Foreign Office, with an additional sprinkling of noblemen among Swedish diplomatic representatives abroad.[21]

Terms of appointment are formally related to posts in the Swedish civil service, and fall into a number of categories differentiated from one another by the degree of security of tenure involved. The 1965

[20] The best analysis to date of the social background of Swedish civil servants is Sten-Sture Landström, Svenska ämbetsmäns sociala ursprung, *Skrifter utgivna av Statsvetenskapliga föreningen i Uppsala*, XXXIV, Almqvist and Wiksell, Uppsala and Stockholm, 1954.

[21] Titles are, however, now no longer in use in the Chancery.

Act enumerated these categories without changing their substance but broke new ground by laying down the general rule that a Civil Service Certificate should be issued to those appointed to non-temporary posts (i.e. to posts created for a period of longer than 3 months).

The difficulty, since the 1965 Act as also before it, is that the legal forms governing terms of appointment to posts are a wavering and unclear guide to practice in some respects. For example, a general distinction is drawn between offices for which budgetary provision is expected to be made year after year (*ordinarie tjänster*) and offices not in this category (*icke-ordinarie tjänster*).[22] Civil servants in the first group are not entitled to resign; those in the second group are free to resign after due notice has been given. In practice, though, a request from a civil servant in the former category to be released from his post will not be refused unless there is difficulty in filling the vacancy. In any case, the principle dividing the two categories is often compromised in practice: offices which are expected to continue in being can be liquidated at need, while those which are more provisional in character may continue undisturbed over a long period of time.

It is not necessary in the present context to become involved in all the subtleties governing terms of appointment in the Swedish civil service, but one or two points may be of interest. Reference was earlier made to the fact that the 1809 Constitution gave most civil servants complete security of tenure in their posts save after trial and conviction in a court of law. This degree of security is still formally enjoyed by higher-ranking civil servants who are appointed under letters patent (*fullmakt*). The duty to resign upon reaching pensionable age was brought about by being written into the Civil Service Pay Regulations (SAAR), and it was squared with the irremovability clause on the grounds that acceptance of the Pay Regulations was voluntary—but, of course, no acceptance—no pay. The duty to accept transfer to another post was also brought about by the use of this same device long before the basic rules were taken out of the

[22] Offices in the second group are not the same as temporary posts created for up to 3 months only.

Constitution in 1965: the Civil Service Act of that year merely recognized existing practice by laying down an obligation on civil servants generally to accept transfer to other posts in accordance with instructions issued by the Government.

Many offices, especially in the trading agency sector, are filled by a form of appointment which allows of dismissal for incompetence in office (appointment by *konstitutorial*). The rationale is clear enough, but the distinction between this and appointment by letters patent is rarely of any practical significance. Some posts, again, are terminable upon 3 months' notice from the employing agency; others, upon 1 month's notice; others—where special need for flexibility is felt—are terminable summarily, like the higher posts in the Chancery. Nor does this exhaust the variety. Some appointments (like, as we have seen, the director-generalships of boards) are made for fixed but renewable terms: during the terms full security of tenure is enjoyed. A few are made for fixed and non-renewable terms. Many, as was mentioned, can be created at need on a temporary basis, not to exceed 3 months' duration. Then there are the probationary (*aspirant*) appointments, the period of probation varying with the post, but commonly lasting 18 months. Still other forms can be discerned: it is enough here to illustrate the range.

It will be clear from what has just been said that Swedish governments have many expedients from which to choose when creating new establishments. It will not, perhaps, be clear how the existence of posts filled on a readily terminable lease, so to speak, can be reconciled with the description of the Swedish civil service as essentially a career service. The answer is in part, as already indicated, that many of these posts in fact afford a considerable degree of security of tenure: the slow—at times, indeed, not so slow—secular expansion in the activities of the State has made retrenchment programmes exceptional. The certificated civil servant can in fact expect to enjoy security of tenure in the service. He can naturally also carry his accumulated pension rights, etc., with him from one post to the next, even if he has to apply for other higher posts in face of competition (in most cases the competition will be internal to the service). At many points in the system the pay scales are so worked as to provide automatic increments at set intervals for civil servants within the same grade, e.g. after 3, 6 and 9 years' service. Finally, as was pointed out earlier, there are in effect many recognized separate career structures within the system, and seniority counts for much in filling posts at the less exalted levels.

The official side in salary negotiations is looked after by the State Collective Bargaining Board, an agency which was set up in 1965 and which contains among its members the under-secretaries of the Finance and Civil Service Affairs departments. The civil service side, as we have seen, is handled by the relevant unions. Parliament—which has a long-standing interest in these matters through voting the supplies and which had complained of being bypassed by direct negotiations—is given a say in the final settlement via a commission representative of all the major parties and empowered to act on behalf of the parent body. An indication of the way this machinery works in practice was given by the Minister for Civil Service Affairs in the course of the 1966 teachers' pay dispute. The magnitude of the issue was then such that the State Collective Bargaining Board had to keep in close touch with the Government, and the Government in turn consulted the parliamentary commission.

The great majority of civil servants are on a multi-graded pay scale (scale A) with variations according to their geographical location—a so-called "cold station allowance", for example, being paid for service in the far north of the country. The higher ranks have since 1965 been paid according to one or other of two scales (B and C, C being the higher) without geographical variation. Their remuneration could fairly be described as comparatively modest. A few illustrations may be of interest, although of course they can only be taken as very rough guides (the more so since they refer to 1964 levels—they are taken from the *1965 Statskalender*: an addition of about 20 per cent should bring them close to the current figures). A first bureau secretary, who then rated A21–23 in the pay scale hierarchy (it may be noted, incidentally, that he ranks as a member of the higher career but is nevertheless on the lower pay-scale) received at that time the equivalent of something between £2088 and £2340 a year. A *chef de bureau* received from £3756 to £4332;

a permanent secretary £4332; an under-secretary £4628; a provincial governor £5328; and directors-general between £4944 and £7092.

It should be borne in mind when considering these salary levels that pensions are paid to civil servants on a non-contributory basis and that salaries are fixed in the light of this. An overhaul of civil service pensions arrangements was carried out in 1958 in the wake of a wider reform of the national pensions system: the original impetus had, however, come from a committee of inquiry which had been set up 7 years previously, and the measure which was finally put into force represented an agreement reached with the staff associations. The categories of civil servant eligible for pension were expanded to include, for example, those working on at least a half-time basis, provided that they have served a qualifying period (part-time jobs, it should be said, are quite common in certain branches of the service—in telephone exchanges, for example, and in the labour exchange field).

A measure of flexibility is usually allowed in respect of the age for retirement, at least outside the defence sector of the administration.[23] A lower and upper retirement limit is set for each post. The higher posts in general have the higher range—65–66: 60–63 is the rule lower down the scales. Retirement is obligatory at the upper limit, though a point is occasionally stretched if this suits the convenience of the service and if the individual concerned is in good fettle. Thirty years' service is normally required to become eligible for full pension, which is paid at the rate of 65 per cent of terminal salary: it becomes payable when the lower limit for retirement is reached. Three years' service is enough to qualify for a payment on leaving, the amount being naturally scaled in accordance with length of service. Early retirement after a longer period of service—commonly 20 years—may carry a regular pension at less than full rate, and there are special arrangements for sickness and widows' pensions.

The holiday allowance for civil servants, in Sweden as in many

[23] The defence sector includes both military staffs and civilians, some 40,000 or so all told on the Defence Department vote. The basis for Swedish defence is a system of general conscription.

other countries, is rather more generous than that usually enjoyed by those in private employment. The standard range varies from 27 to 45 days a year, depending on age and position on the pay scale. Leave of absence with pay (full or partial) may be granted on compassionate grounds, for sickness, pregnancy, studies designed to improve one's professional qualifications, etc.

A few important general points may be very briefly singled out in summary and conclusion. Firstly, the service is so structured that considerable attention is traditionally given to the nature of the job. Partly because of this, Sweden has been spared anything resembling an amateurs *v.* specialists controversy: stress is placed on recruiting persons with suitable qualifications for the job (one reason why post-entry training has been relatively slow to develop). In any case, specialists are readily given full responsibility as managers and as administrators within their own sectors.[24] Secondly, Sweden has a career service, but one modified by considerable mobility in a few key sectors—notably on the policy-shaping side of Chancery work. Thirdly, considerable attention has been paid lately to the development of the planning function and of planning units. The decentralized nature of the system has on balance probably assisted this by permitting the clear delegation of responsibility and freeing the topmost echelons for the scanning of wider and farther horizons. Fourthly, the socio-economic background of higher civil servants in the departments and in many boards (the trading agencies being a major exception in this respect) reveals a mildly elitist state of affairs—which may well change in response to changes in the educational system. Fifthly, the patterns of administrative procedure and the decentralized structure have encouraged a tradition of individual responsibility within the civil service and made it easier to pin-point responsibility for decisions taken.

[24] Much useful information on the position of specialists and others in the Swedish civil service will be found in the essay by Henry Parris on Sweden, in F. F. Ridley (ed.), *Specialists and Generalists*, Allen & Unwin, London, 1968.

CHAPTER 5

The Legislative Process

THE introduction of a unicameral system in 1970, which now has been decided upon, will naturally leave its mark on the legislative process. The system of parliamentary standing committees, for example, will have to be recast in a less distinctive mould. Under present arrangements the two co-equal chambers have equal representation on each of these standing committees; committee reports are—theoretically, at least—debated simultaneously and hence independently in each Chamber; draft Bills lapse if the committees cannot reach agreement after exhausting the standard procedures which they have evolved in order to try and avoid deadlock; and financial measures are settled by means of a joint vote of the two Houses. The disappearance of the Upper House—indirectly elected for an 8-year term by provincial and major city councils, one-eighth retiring annually—and the reshaping of the Lower House into a national legislature along the lines sketched out in the introductory chapter of this book will entail the scrapping of these devices.

Despite these changes, many important features of the Swedish legislative process will remain unaltered. Inter-party agreement has, for example, been reached on the future shape of the parliamentary standing committee system: the principle of specialization will be maintained, and the existing division of labour between the committees will be largely preserved. It is proposed to increase the size of the committees in most cases so as to provide 218 full places in a Chamber with a total membership of 350 (as compared with the current figure of 178 places—excluding deputy members—for a total of 384 *Riksdagsmen*). Each committee will have an odd number of members: this will abate the need for the expedient—not uncommon recently because of the political balance within the chambers—of settling deadlocks in an evenly divided committee by the casting of lots. Again, and leaving aside for the moment the subject of the parliamentary standing committee system, there seems little reason to doubt that commissions of inquiry will continue to be heavily relied upon for the moulding of reforms; that reform proposals will continue to be circulated to the administrative agencies concerned, and to the appropriate major organizations in the field, for open criticism and comment; and that, despite the disciplined nature of the party system, Parliament will continue to enjoy considerable opportunity to make its presence felt as a distinct entity.

Under the 1809 Instrument of Government—still formally in force (until further notice) in this respect—the legislative function is in part shared between Government and Parliament, in part reserved to the Government alone. The 1809 Constitution could be described in general terms as a variation of the classical separation of powers pattern to suit Swedish circumstances and traditions. Thus it enacted that "joint legislation" requiring the consent of both King and Parliament was to comprise "general civil and criminal laws, and criminal laws for the armed forces".[1] Laws regulating the affairs of the established (Lutheran) Church also required the consent of both King and Parliament, and in addition that of the Synod of the Church.[2] Legislation regulating "the general economy of the realm . . . and the principles underlying public institutions of all kinds"—collectively, and rather loosely, styled "economic legislation" in official parlance—was, on the other hand, to be the King's preserve: the Riksdag could make representations in this sector, but it could not do more.[3] This harks back to an older paternalistic view of government in accordance with which the general safety and prosperity of the realm were entrusted to the King. As it stands, it is clearly an anachronism. What has in fact happened is that successive governments have made use of the power given them by the Constitution to transfer matters from the category of

[1] RF, article 87, § 1. [2] *Ibid.*, § 2. [3] *Ibid.*, article 89.

"economic" to that of joint legislation without needing to resort to constitutional amendment. "Economic legislation" has thus contracted to a small and rather ill-defined area which can probably be not unfairly described in general terms as comprising chiefly the making of regulations affecting the administrative system in normal times together with a limited right to make emergency regulations at other times (e.g. during the two world wars). The complexities are a matter for the constitutional lawyer,[4] and the situation is in any case likely to be changed shortly as part of the process of constitutional overhaul. In what follows, therefore, the legislative process will be understood to refer to the making of laws with the co-operation of Parliament, though the discussion can legitimately be enlarged to include government propositions and parliamentary motions.

The Government submits on average about 200 propositions a year for parliamentary consideration.[5] By no means all of these, however, can be reckoned as Bills in the normal sense: many contain proposals for expenditure and for raising revenue which supplement and clarify the annual statement on the condition and requirements of the administration sent in to the Riksdag in January, at the very beginning of the session, as Proposition No. 1 (*statsverkspropositionen*). In the case of important and complex reforms, again, two propositions are commonly submitted: the first contains the financial implications of the measure, the second the legal text. Each proposition may well comprise a small volume in itself, because the supporting documentation is very considerable. It is possible that the weight of written material might decrease if ministers were to be given free access to the meetings of the parliamentary standing committees. But the tradition of setting out the rationale of every measure at length is very strong, and the process of circulating reform projects for comment by interested administrative and private agencies, and incorporating these comments in the draft, stimulates reasoned discussion and reasoned reaction. No

[4] Malmgren, *op. cit.*, pp. 95–97, is one useful commentary.

[5] 1959–64, annual average 197·6 propositions and messages—the latter being very few in number.

draft, of course, can cover every contingency, and so the Government is empowered to issue regulations within the general framework approved by Parliament.

The shape in which a major reform project is laid before the Riksdag may be illustrated by reference to the propositions containing the plans for the nationalization of the police forces of the country in 1964.[6] The first of these propositions, opening with a short summary of the projected reform, ran to 445 pages; the second, opening with the text of the draft Bill, ran to 242 pages. Everything in each proposition after the introductory section is given the fictitious form of an extract from the minutes of the Council of State recording the presentation of the measure by the relevant minister (the Minister of the Interior in this case). The first proposition outlined the early history of the reform project—which included the approval by the Riksdag of a 1962 proposition asking for agreement to be given in principle to the nationalization of police forces in 1965 and the subsequent setting up of a commission of inquiry to work out a detailed scheme. It then took the reform proposals section by section—the organization of the police in the localities, in the regions, and at the national level, etc. Within each section the main recommendations of the commission of inquiry were given a reasoned summary, followed by a condensed reasoned summary of the views of the numerous administrative authorities, professional associations, etc., consulted for an official opinion in accordance with constitutional requirement.[7] At the end of each section the Minister of the Interior drew the threads together from the Government's point of view and came in with a recommendation. Finally, after all the sections had been dealt with in this way, came the heads of agreement reached with the relevant staff associations in connection with the reorganization of personnel and changes in pay structure involved in the reform, followed by the detailed finance proposals. The second proposition—after setting out the draft legal text—gave a detailed analysis of the legal impli-

[6] Propositions, 1964: 100 and 101. Besides nationalizing the police, these measures recast the system of public prosecutors, bailiffs, etc.

[7] RF, article 10.

cations of the reform, not least in the light of its impact upon local government authorities, and went on to provide a clause by clause commentary on the legal changes entailed by the measure. At the end came a brief report from the Law Council with suggestions for textual changes and a note of the action taken by the Government in consequence.

The Law Council (*Lagrådet*), it should be said at this point, is a high-powered advisory agency on the technical legal aspects of draft legislation. For long it consisted of three Supreme Court judges plus one Supreme Administrative Court judge, but it has recently been expanded successively by the addition of extra sections to meet the burden of work. Members serve on a 2-year basis; business is usually presented before the Council by the head of the legal staff in the relevant department of State; and appropriate legal experts can be brought in *ad hoc* when specialist knowledge is required. The Law Council must be heard on all draft joint legislation and the Government has the right to consult it at will on other draft texts—e.g. constitutional amendments.

Parliamentary party meetings normally occur weekly during Riksdag sessions and decide on a party line on important matters pending: the agenda is prepared by the 12 15 members of the parliamentary party executive, though any member of the parliamentary party can raise matters for discussion. Group loyalty is relied upon for adherence to agreed decisions in preference to formal codes of discipline and it appears to prove just as effective.[8] Thus, though no decision is taken on the principle of Bills in the Riksdag itself before the committee stage, committee members will usually feel morally bound by decisions taken in their respective parliamentary groups. On matters of detail there is a little more room for flexibility, though even here the parliamentary party bureaux and specialized party committees are active initiators. Nevertheless, the nature of the standing committee system in the Riksdag increases the scope for effective free discussion.

[8] On parties in Parliament, see N. Andrén, *Modern Swedish Government*, pp. 35–37; E. Håstad, *The Parliament of Sweden*, pp. 122–5 and *Partierna i regering och Riksdag*, pp. 17–59; and Rustow, *op. cit.*, pp. 165–72.

There are at present ten parliamentary standing committees: the committees on Foreign Affairs, the Constitution, Agriculture, Banking, Laws (there are three of these at the moment—Nos. 1, 2, and 3 simply—with the prospect of a fourth), and Miscellaneous Affairs, and the Committees of Supply and of Ways and Means.[9] The basic structure dates from the 1809 Constitution and was tailored to meet parliamentary functions as set out under the modified separation of powers scheme. The terms of reference of the committees were inserted into the Instrument of Government—an unusually rigid device. With the appearance of new committees (also regulated by the Constitution), no clear principle can be discerned behind the present-day division of labour between committees.

Only two of the committees—Agriculture and Foreign Affairs—run parallel to a department of State, and both of these are comparatively new (1909 and 1937 respectively). The constitution-makers of 1809 were not anxious, in view of the experiences of the Era of Liberty, to allow Parliament or its agencies to concern themselves with the workings of the administration except as part of the normal function of long-range supervision. In that function, it may be mentioned in passing, three of the committees are associated: the (1st) Committee on Laws, which was to examine the reports of the Ombudsman; the Committee on the Constitution, which receives the minutes of the Council of State; and the Committee of Supply, to which the reports of the Parliamentary Auditors were assigned.[10] But the dominant task of the committees is the examination of the propositions sent in by the Government and of the motions tabled in the Riksdag. Not all draft legislation, it should be added, goes to the Committees on Laws. The 1st Committee on Laws handles civil, criminal, and ecclesiastical law drafts; the 2nd deals with social

[9] Titles after Thorelli, *op. cit.* The standing committees are discussed at greater length in my article, The parliamentary role of joint standing committees in Sweden, *American Political Science Review*, **45** (June 1951), 464–73 (and also in my unpublished B.Litt. thesis, The system of standing committees of the Swedish Riksdag, Oxford, 1954).

[10] These supervisory activities are discussed in Chapter 7.

and industrial welfare Bills; the 3rd specializes in land law, water rights, fishing rights, etc. But Bills concerning the powers of local government authorities, for example, go to the Committee on the Constitution, Bills concerning alcoholic drinks go to the Committee of Ways and Means, etc.

The committees vary in size at the moment from 16 to 30,[11] but the largest of them—the Committee of Supply—works in specialized sub-groups, and so do one or two of the others. The parties are represented on committee in rough proportion to their strengths in the Riksdag as a whole (it will be recalled that each Chamber for the present has equal committee representation.) This has meant that the Communists were long debarred from committee work—until 1965, to be precise, when they were allotted a place (lost in 1968) in the education sub-group of the Committee of Supply. Committee chairmen are not, by convention, the monopoly of the ruling party—a reflection of the spirit in which the system is worked by the four major political groups. Members are elected for one year at a time and re-election is the rule. Since electoral landslides are rare in Sweden, an MP can in very many cases look forward to a reasonably long parliamentary life. The consequence is that committee members often come to know one another well. Informality is aided by the fact that the proceedings are held in private.

Expert assistance is made available to each committee on technical points by its secretariat, which commonly occupies an office next door to the committee rooms. The secretariat is a small organization consisting of a secretary in charge and anything between one and a score or so of others on the staff. The members were provided till 1966 from newer members of the higher ranks of the administration and the courts—and, naturally enough, they were usually drawn from sectors of particular relevance to the work of the committee. Thus the Committee on Agriculture liked to draw upon the Department of Agriculture, the Ways and Means Committee on the Tax Appeals Court, the Law Committees on the Courts of Appeal, and so on. In some committees the secretary was reappointed for many

[11] Full members. There are also deputy members, but they can fairly be left out of account in the present context.

years, in others the turnover was rapid—the post was often regarded as a useful staging point by those aspiring to the higher peaks of the service.

Many on the secretariat staffs (though not all) were entirely freed from administrative duties in order to be able to give their full attention to committee work: they returned to their departments when the Riksdag went into recess—provided, of course, that their committee did not have to meet during the recess (which was exceptional). Quite often it happened that the secretariat official had been involved in shaping a measure at the pre-parliamentary stage: he was then in a particularly good position to answer questions on its technical aspects. Since 1966 the employment of Chancery officials on secondment by committees has been generally discontinued, and the committees have switched over to full-time staffs of their own. Measures are presented to committee by the secretary or by a senior staff member. Sometimes—not least when the work-load of the secretariat is high towards the end of a session—permission is sought for an outside official who has been concerned with a measure, maybe as secretary to a commission of inquiry, to carry out the presentation. Sometimes, again, permission is sought for an outside official to appear before the committee in order to answer questions, or perhaps to give additional information. On the whole the committees prefer to rely on their own staffs whenever they can. The chief duties of the secretariat are, as one might expect, to provide expert assistance, to keep the minutes, and to write up the draft reports of their committees: they do not take part in committee deliberations proper. It may be added that state grants have, since 1966, gone out to parliamentary party groups—at a higher rate to non-government parties than to the Social Democrats—to help them with their research facilities.

The committees, thus aided, produce a modest flow of successful amendments to the Bills and finance proposals put before them. MPs occasionally make effective use of their right to propose increases of expenditure, for example—though naturally the changes allowed are of little or no overall financial significance. Thus, to give a few concrete illustrations from recent years, a joint Liberal–

Centre Party amendment to a national health insurance proposition won some Social Democratic support in committee and led to an increase in maternity benefits: the Committee of Supply successfully accepted an increase in the vote for the welfare of handicapped persons; the grant to fisheries was raised by 30,000 kronor; a subsidy to small farmers was continued beyond the time-limit originally intended for it; and an administrative assistant not originally budgeted for was voted for the African Institute at the University of Uppsala. Some of these detailed amendments have attracted general support on the merits of the case; others (especially before the 1968 elections) have squeezed through on a joint vote of the two Chambers after winning on the luck of the draw in an evenly divided committee; others again were the product of a compromise engineered in committee after the two Chambers have differed.

All this has helped to keep up the spirits of the opposition parties and to preserve the image of the Riksdag as a legislature with a taste for detail—an image which finds an accurate reflection in the prevailing style of speech-making. But the fact remains that the resources available to the Government for shaping its proposals are far greater than those available to Parliament for reviewing them. The weight of detail is at busy times so great as to be overmastering. the business of presentation then can serve as a welcome means of digesting the mass. On the whole, the spirit of *saklighet* finds its greatest scope in dealing with Riksdag rather than with government initiatives.

Parliamentary motions may cost committee secretariats more labour than propositions, especially when they seem to contain the germ of a good idea repaying research (more often still, they receive summary treatment, but this is by the way). It is in this connection that the committees occasionally put into operation the complicated procedure formally laid down for extracting information from the departments and boards. Strictly speaking, a committee is expected to apply for information through its chairman (not its secretary) to a minister specially designated for the purpose each Riksdag by the King (=the Government). The Minister then passes on the request to his colleagues in Council and, if it is approved, the department or board concerned is asked in the name of the King to surrender the desired information. The point of this elaborate routine is to safeguard the independence of the administration. It is, in fact, normally used only when the committee is anxious to obtain a comprehensive written report on a motion. Recently committees have been urged to avoid burdening the administration with investigations on their behalf and to rely more on their own secretariat resources. Permission for civil servants to speak in committee is sought via a legal Minister without Portfolio.

The Riksdag is very active in taking the initiative with finance and other proposals. The number of private members' motions submitted in the Upper House during the years 1959–64 inclusive averaged 759 a year, while the corresponding annual average in the Lower House was 920. In both cases, moreover, a steady annual increase was recorded—from 613 in the Upper House in 1959 to 893 in 1964, and from 726 in the Lower House in 1959 to 1103 in 1964. In 1967 and 1968 the upward trend continues. The totals are formidable and require some explanation.

Firstly, a great many motions are tabled in connection with government propositions and are to be regarded as draft amendments on points of detail. Many of these are shaped in the parliamentary offices and the specialized committees of the opposition parties and, as has been seen, they may suggest not only amendments to draft Bills but also the upwards or downwards revision of finance proposals (including revenue proposals). Secondly, there is often a tendency for the years immediately preceding a general election to produce record totals. From this point of view the 1959–64 period was atypical—1961/2 produced higher totals than 1960. But certainly the sharp rise in political tensions in 1967/8 is reflected in the aggregates. This has a connection with another, more important, point: motions are very often couched in the form of invitations to the Riksdag to send petitions to the Government asking for an inquiry to be launched into the subject raised, with a view to reform. Encouragement is thus given to opposition parties and individual backbenchers to put all kinds of projects into circulation. An infinite variety results, and also a considerable parliamentary industry. Topics mooted for investigation in recent years have ranged from the injuries caused by boxing to the need for a new morality and have included just about everything in between. Some motions are recurrent and meet the same fate year by year until at last, perhaps, they are successful. The annual carnage is always very heavy although, as the late Professor Håstad put it, motions "cannot be left to perish on the tables of the Houses nor be killed in committee. . . . Even when motions are rejected they receive a state funeral with the opportunity for graveside speeches from their sponsors and others."[12] The majority of these motions spring from backbench initiatives, but some of the weightier ones are party-sponsored and are undersigned by the party leader and the parliamentary executive. The general totals, it should be added, are somewhat artificially swollen by the fact that many motions (for the present) are tabled in identical terms in each of the two Chambers.

Parties naturally make use of the motion procedure for publicizing their programmes—the Centre Party and the Liberals, for example, made sure that their major joint motions in the period before the 1968 elections were launched with suitable press coverage. Sometimes, inevitably, there is a "jam to-morrow" flavour about some of the motions calling for inquiries tabled as an election draws near, e.g. motions mooting the possibility of lowering the age for the payment of state pensions, or of exempting old-age pensioners from the payment of taxes, or of increasing state grants to local authorities for one purpose and another. At the same time the opposition parties, acting under the influence of the same stimulus, went to the trouble of incorporating into motions their various sets of budget proposals before the 1968 elections so that the electorate could see where they stood.

Not all motions, of course, are what they seem: motions for inquiries, in particular, are useful for cooling political hot potatoes or otherwise for avoiding issues until they cease to be relevant (and the award of an inquiry by the Government can, for that matter, serve similar purposes). But some motions, at the end of the day, give rise in their turn to government propositions and thus afford

[12] E. Håstad, *The Parliament of Sweden*, p. 101.

the back-bench sponsor the feeling that he has achieved something worthwhile. The value of the parliamentary motion as a kind of suggestion-box device is not to be underrated. The Riksdag likes to think of itself as an unspectacular hard-working legislature: in this field especially there is substance in the belief.

The Constitution imposes time-limits on the submission of both propositions and motions in an effort to regulate the flow of work. The financial year starts on 1 July. Propositions containing finance proposals, therefore, "shall be presented to the Riksdag within seventy days from its opening, and, with the exception of propositions concerning the final settlement of the budget . . . may not be presented later unless the King [=Government] considers that delay in presenting . . . would cause serious detriment to the public interest".[13] The general finance plan for the year is, as indicated earlier, always the first proposition to be submitted, and in connection with it a large-scale general debate occurs on government policy which corresponds roughly to the Debate on the Address in Britain and lasts for two or three days. Propositions of a non-financial character are not quite so tightly regulated. They "ought" to be within 90 days of the opening of Parliament "unless the King considers that delay in presenting . . . would cause detriment to the public interest or otherwise finds that special reasons call for . . . presentation".[14] In practice there is a marked tendency for a considerable number of propositions to be handed in towards the end of the time-limit and for a sizeable backlog to come in late—in 1967, a bad year from this point of view, some 50 or so were notified to the Riksdag as pending on 30 March. Situations of this kind lead to much parliamentary grumbling and to the choking of committee agendas in late spring. Propositions not containing finance proposals may, however, be postponed from the spring to an autumn session of Parliament, and they may then be postponed again if need be until the next year's Riksdag—when they must be finally decided, either in spring or in autumn. It follows from the constitutional rules that the government may submit propositions for the first time at the autumn session if the public interest or some special

[13] RO, article 54. [14] *Ibid.*

reason requires this. Autumn sessions have been the rule since 1949, but it remains true that the bulk of parliamentary business is disposed of in the spring.

Constitutional amendments are, as one might expect, subject to more exacting rules than ordinary propositions. The key requirement is that they must be approved by two separate parliaments, so that a general election must intervene between initiation and ratification. Since the Lower House is elected for a 4-year term, this means that, under present arrangements, almost 8 years *could* elapse before an amendment goes through (after 1970 this would be cut to 6 years). But in practice amendments—which are frequent—are usually tabled towards the end of one legislature and passed, or passed over, at the beginning of the next. It can hardly be said that the device of ensuring that they go before the electorate in this way results in a reliable popular verdict on their merits, since they are commonly submerged by the more bread-and-butter issues of the campaign. In this connection the 1963 Commission on the Constitution unsuccessfully proposed that a constitutional amendment should be made subject to a consultative referendum at the same time as a general election if a third of the Riksdag gave this their support.

Consultative referenda, it may be mentioned in passing, were written into the Swedish Constitution in 1922 at the time of the campaign for prohibition, and a referendum was first used later that same year in order to test public opinion on the issue (the "Drys" lost). The institution then languished: it was not employed again until 1955, when there was an overwhelming vote in favour of retaining left-hand driving on the roads (subsequently reversed by inter-party agreement). The last instance was in 1957, on pensions schemes. A Bill must be passed through Parliament before a consultative referendum can be held.

Motions, like propositions, are subject to time-limits, and in this case the regulations are more severe. The general rule is that motions shall be tabled within 15 days of the submission of the annual finance plan to Parliament in January. The whole of this period is often found necessary to deliberate on what matters to raise—witness the fact that 385 Upper House and 466 Lower House motions were tabled on the fifteenth day in 1966. Motions tabled in conjunction with propositions (amendment motions) are normally required to be handed in within 10 days of the arrival of the proposition, but the House may grant an extension of up to 5 days "owing to intervening holidays or the extraordinary magnitude of the matter concerned".[15] Motions immediately related to developments occurring during the Riksdag may be submitted as long as the Riksdag is in session. The same applies to the relatively small category of motions on questions affecting one House only.

Motions, as was mentioned earlier, are one important source of the inquiries which are commonly used to pave the way for legislative change in Sweden. The original impulse towards an inquiry comes most often, however (as one might expect), from within the executive itself—especially from the Government and the departments of State, but sometimes, too, from the administrative agencies which are expected to keep abreast of new developments in their field and to come in with suggestions for reform. Apart from these sources, the initial suggestion may also be made by a local government authority, an interest group, an existing inquiry working on a related subject, or even a private individual. In some of these cases (and virtually always in the case of opposition party instances) the suggestion may crystallize out in the form of a parliamentary motion—but a direct approach to the relevant department is often preferred. Government approval is naturally required before an inquiry can be launched, and a powerful and flexible instrument is thus secured to governments for the shaping of public policy.

The large scale of the inquiry system in Sweden can be seen partly as a reflection of a general readiness to make civil servants individually responsible for technical policy recommendations, partly as a reflection of the small size of the departments of State. About 300–400 inquiries are active as a rule at any one time, and their annual budget—which is borne on the votes of the relevant departments—runs to roughly £2 million. A large minority—rather more than one-third—are one-man affairs, and are commonly carried out by a civil servant in a responsible position with the help of a group

[15] RO, article 55.

of experts designated by the Minister for the task. The experts may come from within the public service or outside it (they often represent interest groups, for example): standing advisory committees are relatively uncommon in the Swedish system, and this arrangement may be regarded as an *ad hoc* equivalent. Thus, to illustrate the point, a civil servant with legal qualifications was carrying out an inquiry in 1964 into the operation of a law of 1954 concerning the education and care of mentally handicapped children with the help of seven experts, including an inspector of special schools, two headmasters, a professor of medicine and a director of child care services; another one-man inquiry simultaneously in progress on the subject of the laws relating to domestic service had the assistance of four advisers, among them a vice-president of the Swedish Housewives' League and a woman MP from the Lower House. Inquiries such as these may in many cases be regarded chiefly as a device to enable departments to carry out their normal work with increased efficiency. But one-man inquiries, it should be added, are by no means always conducted by officials: MPs in particular are quite often called upon, sometimes from the ranks of the opposition. In 1964, to cite a random example, an MP was investigating the training given to national servicemen: he had fourteen experts to help him in the task.

Most inquiries are multi-member affairs—some consisting purely of civil servants, some of MPs, some of a mixture of both with perhaps interest group representatives added. The variations in composition are considerable and the comparatively small manpower resources available in the departments are thus supplemented by help from outside—not only on the commissions of inquiry themselves, but also in the experts who are drafted to assist the proceedings (they may be "experts" only in the sense of representing an affected interest). The terms of reference of all inquiries require formal authorization by the Council of State (they are, in particular, subject to scrutiny by the relevant Minister without Portfolio and also by the Departments of Finance and of Civil Service Affairs). They usually take the form of a statement by the Minister at the head of the department most closely concerned with the inquiry and they are written up within that department. They may be drawn narrowly or broadly as the Government sees fit. Whether or not the Cabinet is involved in the selection of members depends largely on the political importance of the inquiry: in many cases the size of the commission is fixed by the Cabinet and the relevant Minister is left free to make the appointments (Cabinet lunches in any event provide a convenient opportunity for any consultation that might be desired, e.g. about a chairmanship). When interest group representation is sought, it is common practice for the Minister to approach the executive of the group concerned and to ask for a nomination. The same pattern is usually followed when opposition party representation as such is desired: in other cases a direct approach is often made to the MP concerned.

The Under-Secretaries of departments are much used for the chairmanship of important inquiries, and so are some Directors-General of boards and Provincial Governors (it is not uncommon for certain key personalities holding these offices to be active on several inquiries at the same time). Occasionally a Minister may take on the task himself, occasionally it may be given to an opposition MP, sometimes to a member of the government majority in the Riksdag. Secretarial assistance is provided subject to the approval and at the charge of the department concerned: a younger civil servant is often chosen, drawn from an appropriate board, or sometimes from the department itself. Experts are frequently appointed at the suggestion of the inquiry, though formally designated by the Minister. Inquiries containing MPs among their members, it may be added, often find it convenient to meet in late summer or autumn when the Riksdag is in recess—hence the well-known "seaside resort conferences".

Inquiry proceedings are traditionally thorough, reports are often voluminous, and operations are as likely as not to last beyond the span of a year. A commission of five, for instance, was appointed in 1958 to investigate the relationship between the Established (Lutheran) Church and the State—it was headed by a judge of the Supreme Court and consisted otherwise of a bishop, a headmaster, a TUC official, and a Social Democratic clergyman from the Lower

House. It delivered a series of eleven reports, totalling over 3000 pages, on various aspects of its subject-matter—the last of them in 1968. An inquiry of six with a strong university element (and one MP—a Social Democrat) was appointed in 1961 to investigate the concentration of ownership in the private sector of the economy: it reported at length early in 1968. Another weighty and long-lived commission was appointed in 1958 under the chairmanship of a senior Finance Ministry official to study and report on various aspects of social welfare policies. Its ten members included two Social Democratic MPs, one of them a woman doctor and the other with experience of labour exchange work; a Centre Party MP, a Liberal MP with experience of social work, and a schoolteacher who had been a Conservative MP; and also two union officials and another high-ranking civil servant. The chairman became Under-Secretary to the Department of the Interior in 1964 and was succeeded for the final stages of the inquiry by Ernst Michanck who, as Under-Secretary to the Department of Social Welfare, had been a prominent authority in this field for some time. These are a few of many examples which might be given of the major inquiries, analogous to royal commissions, whose work can span several years. Inquiries of this type, it may be added in conclusion, along with the parliamentary standing committees, helped governments to remain productive during the era of minority rule in the 1920s. The proportion of MPs appointed to inquiries was increased;[16] governments, by convention, did not disband inquiries appointed by their predecessors; and, despite a tendency to over-represent small centre of gravity groups, agreed policies were thus facilitated in advance of parliamentary debate. Agreed policies, incidentally, remain very much the ideal within the inquiry system, although minority reports are permissible and not infrequent.

Once an inquiry has reported, the next stage is the circulation of the report for written comment to administrative agencies and (where appropriate) major interest groups. "Before matters are submitted to the King in Council", as the Instrument of Government

[16] H. Meijer, *Kommittépolitik och kommittäarbete*, Gleerup, Lund, 1956, pp. 69 *et seq.*

puts it, "they shall be prepared by the member submitting them, who shall collect for this purpose the necessary information from the competent administrative offices."[17] The relevant department is thus made responsible for deciding whose opinion should be sought (the Under-Secretary usually plays an important part in making out the list): it often takes into account suggestions made to it by the chairman or secretary of the inquiry.

This "remiss" stage, as it is called, is, of course, designed to make sure that all available expertise is brought to bear on reform proposals at the formative phase and that the most important bodies likely to be affected by a measure are brought into consultation while consultation can still be effective. To some extent it still succeeds in this: the proposals put forward by inquiries are often modified on detailed points (and occasionally shelved completely) as a result of the arguments that are later brought to bear. Thus in spring 1967, to give one example, a scheme to close the state monopoly shops selling wines and spirits on Saturdays and the eve of holidays in exchange for lengthening their retailing hours two evenings a week was abandoned after coming in for criticism on remiss. The remiss procedure also ensures that official views divergent from those of the Government are given a public airing, sometimes adding to the opposition's armoury in the process.

Practice, however, frequently falls short of the ideal. The circulation of draft proposals and of inquiry recommendations to interested parties slows down the legislative time-table and contributes to parliamentary grumblings about the late submission of quantities of propositions. To counter this, recourse is sometimes had to the imposition of strict time-limits on the return of answers to government requests for formal opinions. In 1967, for example, a fortnight was allowed for comments to be made on the important draft scheme for a state investment bank. Again, some administrative agencies and public authorities tend to get swamped at times by requests for their opinions. It is not long since the Organization and Methods Office was particularly hard-hit in this respect, and the federations representative of local authority units

[17] RF, article 10.

can be cited as instances of bodies whose views are constantly in demand.

On the whole, though—and despite some points of friction of the type outlined in the last paragraph—the Swedish legislative process can fairly be characterized in general terms as leisurely, thorough, and (from the back-bencher's point of view) relatively liberal.

CHAPTER 6

Internal and Judicial Controls on the Executive

JUDICIAL control of an administrative system is an external control and so ought strictly to fall within the scope of the next chapter of this study. But it is closely linked with the question of the civil servant's liability for his actions and therefore may be considered here under that head in conjunction with disciplinary proceedings. The work of the Ombudsmen, which is also closely connected with the question of civil service liability, is dealt with in the next chapter along with a number of other parliamentary checks on the administration. The absence of the principle of ministerial responsibility for civil service actions is obviously significant in this general context.

The administrative appeal serves partly as a means of ensuring that administrative decisions affecting an individual interest have been taken with a proper regard for the relevant formal procedures. More generally, it is also the standard method for resolving disputes concerning the exercise of administrative discretion in matters affecting an individual interest, e.g. tax appeal and national insurance cases. Not surprisingly, therefore, administrative appeals are commonly heard by bodies which, although in Sweden they go by the name of administrative courts, are in reality closely akin over much of the field to administrative tribunals. Here again we might appear to be concerned with a control of an external nature, but the Swedes on the whole prefer the contrary classification partly because of the influence of the doctrine of the separation of powers (a point which is discussed below, in connection with administrative appeals generally), and partly because the appeals system functions in a real sense as an internal safeguard of administrative coherence and uniformity.

The work of the Ombudsmen, it should perhaps be said at this point, is principally linked to the abuse of administrative discretion and to administrative malpractices of various kinds. We are here in the realms of *détournement de pouvoir*, of bias, negligence, etc.—in short, of a whole complex of varieties of maladministration which are neatly comprehended under the offence of "dereliction of duty" at Swedish law (this is discussed below). Persons aggrieved by decisions of this kind may prefer to seek a remedy through the administrative courts over much of the field, but in some instances the Ombudsmen alone can provide the hope of redress—and in addition the Ombudsmen make regular use of their right to recommend changes in malfunctioning laws and unsatisfactory administrative procedures in the light of their investigations.

THE CIVIL SERVANT'S LIABILITY FOR HIS ACTIONS

Civil servants in the departments are not legally liable for breach of official duty when taking part in the process of helping to shape public policy: formally they are then acting as the advisers of advisers (ministers), and the usual rule of individual responsibility does not apply. Otherwise breaches of official duty expose civil servants, with the exception of those in certain categories of post carrying minimal responsibility,[1] to the possibility of prosecution in the courts for serious cases. For lesser offences disciplinary action may be taken by the authority concerned. Civil servants in the humbler positions mentioned above are subject exclusively to disciplinary action for professional offences and are no more liable to prosecution

[1] E.g. clerical assistants, doorkeepers. The principles underlying the exceptions are in fact rather complex and are not considered at length here in order to avoid involvement in legal subtleties too far afield from the main theme. See, for example, H. Strömberg, *Allmän förvaltningsrätt*, Gleerup, Lund, 1962, p. 63.

in court than any other ordinary citizen. A prosecution cannot be brought against top-ranking officials by an individual citizen who considers that he has suffered as the result of a professional offence: it must be authorized by an official prosecutor—either the Chancellor of Justice (*Justitiekanslern*) or one of the Riksdag's Ombudsmen.

The professional offences which thus entail the possibility of legal proceedings for the great majority of civil servants are set out in the Swedish Penal Code and are widely drawn. The main heads are the taking of bribes, the misuse of official position, the breach of official secrecy and "dereliction of duty" (*tjänstefel*). This last offence occurs when a civil servant is guilty of "failure to perform, through neglect, lack of understanding, or lack of skill, whatever is required of him by law, Instruction, or other regulation or special ordinance or by the nature of his office".[2] Within this area of "dereliction of duty"—where offences are commonly of a less serious as well as of a less deliberate nature—recourse is usually had to disciplinary action for civil servants in the relevant categories. The commentary accompanying the relevant proposition makes it clear that the offence may be interpreted to cover not only, for example, absence without due cause or persistent lateness, but also unmannerly conduct towards the public while at work and even, in some circumstances, behaviour outside office hours likely to bring discredit on the public service.[3]

A civil servant who finds himself faced with disciplinary action has the right to ask for a hearing at which he can call upon a colleague to help defend him—he may well, in fact, call upon a member of his staff association.[4] Minor transgressions may be dealt with by a single official, more serious ones by a disciplinary tribunal—a governing board acts on occasion in this capacity. Whenever several people are involved in adjudicating, the traditional voting

[2] Penal Code, chapter 20, para. 4.

[3] Proposition, 1965: 60, p. 181.

[4] Except in cases involving security considerations, when a lawyer may be asked to serve instead.

procedure must be followed. The permissible standard penalties are laid down by law: a caution (which may affect promotion prospects); deductions from salary for a period of up to 30 days; suspension from office for up to 3 months; and, in extreme cases, dismissal. Civil servants who are appointed by letters patent cannot be dismissed through disciplinary action—only after trial in a court of law. The maximum penalties that may be imposed for professional offences after conviction in a court are heavier than in the case of disciplinary penalties and may include, apart from dismissal, suspension from duty and indeed imprisonment in the worst instances for a period of up to a year. In order to avoid double punishment for the same offence, disciplinary proceedings must lapse in the event of prosecution; and if a disciplinary punishment has been wholly or partly executed before a court case is brought, then the court is required to take this into consideration when passing sentence.

Actions for damages can generally be brought against civil servants in the courts by members of the public who have suffered from wrongful decisions or from negligence. Actions against higher civil servants for damages arising out of professional offences, like other actions in connection with those offences, require the approval of an Ombudsman or of the Chancellor of Justice. State and local government authorities can seek to recover damages from their officials in the courts: they are not themselves financially liable for the consequences of the errors and omissions of officials—or rather, their liability does not extend beyond the usual legal liability of a private firm in respect of its employees.

Within the administration a general surveillance is exercised over civil servants on behalf of the Crown by the Chancellor of Justice, one of whose chief tasks is to see that officials carry out their legal obligations and that administrative behaviour maintains a high standard of correctness.[5] To this end he is required by the Constitution to be "an able, impartial person, versed in the law, who has had

[5] For a fuller (and first-hand) account of the work of this official, see S. Rudholm, The Chancellor of Justice, in D. C. Rowat (ed.), *The Ombudsman*, Allen & Unwin, 1965, pp. 17–22.

experience as a judge".[6] He is bound to investigate all allegations of official misconduct that come to his notice, whether from members of the public or in the Press or in the course of the tours of inspection which he is required to undertake.[7] He is empowered to attend the meetings and deliberations of administrative authorities and of law courts (for judges also fall within his sphere of supervision), and to require the production of all relevant information, including administrative and legal documents and minutes.[8] In all this he performs, from within the administration, a task similar to that performed—with similar powers—by the Ombudsman on behalf of the Riksdag. In the nature of the case, however, he tends to receive fewer complaints than they from members of the public, and to be approached more readily by administrative agencies anxious for an authoritative ruling on the legality of an administrative practice. He keeps in informal touch with the Ombudsmen in order to avoid overlap. Only in a very small minority of instances does he find it necessary to prosecute, being usually "content to let the matter rest once the fault has been put right or an explanation given"[9]—if, that is, he does not shelve it forthwith as not worth investigation. Putting the matter right may involve disciplinary action or simply promising to change a procedure as the result of a criticism. In 1966, for example, in an investigation which attracted considerable attention, the Chancellor of Justice's strictures led to the winding up of a fund which the Commander-in-Chief had had put at his disposal from private sources for various specific purposes—the investigation itself having been originally into the theft of an envelope containing 10,000 kronor from the C.-in-C.'s office. It is also a part of the Chancellor's duties to help avoid administrative bottlenecks caused by understaffing, etc.; for this purpose he receives an annual report from administrative agencies of their work-balances and draws the attention of the Government in his own annual report to authorities with heavy backlogs.

[6] RF, article 27.
[7] *Instruktion för Justitiekanslersämbetet*, paras. 3 and 5.
[8] *Ibid.*, paras. 6 and 7.
[9] *Ibid.*, para 3.

The Chancellor of Justice, finally, has functions analogous to those of an Attorney-General, although he is not a member of the Government.[10] He acts as chief legal adviser to the Government (delivering formal opinions as request on remiss, for example); keeps an eye on the Crown interest in lawsuits, acting as the Crown's representative when necessary; and has a special responsibility for prosecuting offences in breach of the Freedom of the Press Act.[11]

SPECIALIZED AGENCIES FOR INTERNAL FINANCE AND EFFICIENCY CONTROL

1. *The Organization and Methods Office* (*O & M*) (*Statskontoret*)

This agency, which is attached to the Finance Department, is primarily concerned with increasing efficiency and cutting costs within the administration by carrying out work surveys and advising on time- and labour-saving devices and techniques. As a part of this general function it acts as the central authority for the purchase and co-ordination of the use of computers in the public service: it administers a special fund for this purpose and hires out computers to agencies requiring them, besides organizing a variety of training courses in the use of computers and computer work for officials from other branches of the administration. Also as a part of the same general function the O & M Office is expected to scrutinize the estimates of administrative authorities on remiss with a view to securing economies without loss of efficiency when administrative reorganizations are proposed. It is further expected to give a formal opinion at the remiss stage on the reports of inquiries having similar implications. The burden of this remiss work has been so heavy—averaging over 300 formal opinions delivered annually in the early 1960's—that an inquiry reporting on the work of the office just before an overhaul was undertaken in 1965 recommended restraint in the submission of material on the grounds that the systematic

[10] It is chiefly because he is not a member of the Government that the title of Chancellor of Justice is here preferred.

[11] *Tryckfrihetsförordningen*, chapter 9, article 2.

O & M surveys which were the heart of the office's work were suffering in consequence.

The 1965 overhaul of the O & M Office's structure, occurring at the same time as the wider reforms in the organization of the departments of State,[12] was designed to strengthen the agency for undertaking larger-scale "across the board" investigations into functions common to many authorities (registry procedures, for example), and also to permit a greater degree of follow-up work than had hitherto been possible. Thus in 1967 the office produced a report urging the extension of cost-accounting techniques and the revision of budgetary practice by the central administration (the trading agencies had blazed the trail here already). Every administrative authority is required to make its own arrangements and to appoint its own staff, to ensure that its work is efficiently organized: the O & M Office acts as a common service agency advising on the rationalization of office work and training civil servants from other parts of the administration in these skills. It does not, however, perform this function for the entire central administrative system: the defence sector now has its own O & M Office (established in 1968). The trading agencies, too, enjoy a considerable degree of autonomy in O & M matters, the state railways, for instance, having their own highly developed section—though the O & M Office carries out surveys in the trading agency field from time to time.

O & M surveys have come thick and fast in the central administration of recent years. Sometimes the Government commissions them, sometimes an administrative authority, and sometimes they are undertaken on the initiative of the O & M Office itself. The office's recommendations have advisory and not binding effect, and it has inherited the traditions of an earlier (pre-1961) agency in the field[13] and carries out its surveys in co-operation with the relevant authority chiefs. But its recommendations carry great weight, and at the end of the day the Finance Department can make approval for staff increases, for example, dependent upon the adoption of revisions of practice which have been suggested earlier by the office.

[12] And submitted to Parliament in Proposition, 1965: 42.

[13] *Statens organisationsnämnden.*

2. *The National Audit Office* (*Riksrevisionsverket*)

The National Audit Office, which is also attached to the Finance Department, is the agency with general responsibility for scrutinizing the accounts of the central administration. It carries out both a check on the legality of expenditure and an efficiency audit. This latter function involves it in co-operation with the O & M Office, and in fact its Director-General sits as vice-chairman on the latter authority's board while its own vice-chairman is the Director-General of the O & M Office. The main bulk of its accounting work lies in the efficiency audit field and a 1967 reform encouraged this further by strengthening the organization in this sector. It is required in this connection to pay particular attention to seeing that the State gets value for money in its purchases, that good business practice is followed as far as possible when the State engages in economic activity, and that the revenues flow in without unnecessary expense.

Other administrative authorities have their own accounts sections and the trading agencies, for example, scrutinize for themselves the accounts of their own regional and local branches. This does not debar the Audit Office from inspecting any accounts it wishes. Part of the object of the 1967 reforms, however, was to increase the efficiency of internal audit and so leave the Audit Office freer to concentrate on scientific sampling. The office has the power to standardize bookkeeping procedures and, in co-operation with the O & M Office, it has played a large part in the recent computerization of accounting. It also has the power to table criticisms in connection with irregularities it discovers in the accounts. The scope for this has diminished along with concern for the saving of candle-ends, but criticisms may still be made, for example, in connection with irregular payments of public moneys. In such cases it is left to the relevant authority to decide whether or not to seek restitution from the offending official or, in serious cases, whether or not to prosecute him.

In addition to these responsibilities the Audit Office also acts as the agency for compiling financial statistics in the public sector. Thus it keeps a running check on expenditure and revenue levels, forecasts, and charts the final outcome of the budget, and in particular provides annual estimates for the revenue side of the budget.

It should be mentioned in conclusion that the Riksdag has its own auditors for checking the accounts of the central administration: their work is discussed in the next chapter.

ADMINISTRATIVE APPEALS (*BESVÄR*)

The general relationship between the courts of law and the administration in Sweden continues to be regulated in accordance with the separation of powers philosophy underlying the Constitution of 1809. The courts have jurisdiction over civil and criminal offences; their authority to punish civil servants for professional offences may be regarded as a special application of their general jurisdiction in the penal sphere; they enjoy thereby a wide indirect power of control over administrative legality. At the same time, they have no general power directly to quash an administrative decision on the ground of illegality, neither can they command or prohibit the performance of any act by an administrative authority. Parliamentary motions are regularly tabled with the intention of strengthening judicial powers of control, but on the whole practice has moved rather in the direction of strengthening the guarantees of justice within the administrative sector while keeping the executive and judicial arms of government co-ordinate and independent. Against this background the administrative appeal assumes a particular importance.

The main control over administrative decisions, then, is exercised within the administration itself, in part by administrative authorities and in part by administrative courts (or tribunals) which have the formal status of central boards. The broad outlines of the appeals system are comparatively simple, although there are many variations of detail. The right to appeal against an administrative decision belongs to any person whose interest is directly affected by that decision; appeals shall be submitted in writing within the prescribed time, namely 3 weeks; appeals may lie both on grounds of illegality and of inadvisability; they may result in the amendment of the challenged decision or in its annulment; decisions not challenged at the end of the appeal period shall have full validity; clearly unreasonable or improper decisions may subsequently be challenged by recourse to special remedies. These rules apply to appeals against the decisions of central administrative authorities and also those of local government authorities when acting as agents of the State—strictly speaking, the true administrative appeals in the Swedish usage (*förvaltningsbesvär*). It may be mentioned in passing that somewhat different rules apply to appeals against the decisions of local authorities acting within the sphere of local self-government (*kommunalbesvär*). These can only be challenged on the ground of illegality, never of inadvisability; they can only be quashed, never altered; and they may be challenged by any member of the local community in question.

At the apex of the appeals system stands the King—a relic, this, of the right which the Swedish citizen enjoyed from a very early date to "go to the King" when aggrieved by the decisions of those in authority. This no longer signifies, as it used to do in the earliest days of a central administration, that there is one single last instance for the hearing of administrative appeals: there is no appeals system in this sense. Nevertheless, despite the successive devolution of the royal power to hear appeals against administrative decisions to central boards and other administrative authorities, the weight of appeals business continuing to flow in to the Council of State was still so heavy at the beginning of this century that it was decided, in 1909, to set up a Supreme Administrative Court (*Regeringsrätt*) to relieve the pressure. The situation now is, therefore, that the Government and the Supreme Administrative Court share out a number of the most important appeals between them—the Supreme Administrative Court being unique among courts of this type in ranking as an offshoot of the Council of State.

The basic division of labour between the Government and the Supreme Administrative Court is laid down by statute. The subjects with which the court may deal are enumerated, the Government may take the rest. Adjustments of detail are made annually. Roughly speaking, the Court handles those appeals which primarily involve legal considerations, the Government handles those which primarily involve questions of advisability. All appeals of a character to "go to the King" are first sent in to the relevant department of State and assigned either for court or government decision by the Permanent Secretary. The preparation of cases for consideration by the Court is in the hands of departmental specialists who also present the case in court and expedite the final decision. The preparation of cases for consideration by the Government is usually a fairly routine matter and is handled accordingly within the department.

Only two-thirds of the members of the Supreme Administrative Court have to be qualified as judges, the rest are administrators. Cases may be heard by five judges or by four, in which latter event three must agree upon a verdict for a valid result. Among the types of case decided by the Court are appeals by civil servants against disciplinary punishments; cases involving the principle of the publicity of official documents; certain categories of tax appeals (the most numerous of all); electoral cases;[14] and appeals against local government decisions within the sphere of local self-government (when, it will be remembered, the main issue is one of the legality of the decision). In some instances local government authorities have to submit decisions for approval by a state authority (commonly a provincial government): appeals against the decision of the state authority usually go to the Supreme Administrative Court for an opinion, but, since policy matters are involved, the final decision is reserved to the Government. The Government handles a miscellaneous assortment of appeals of this type, e.g. appeals against local traffic regulations or against provincial government public order and safety regulations. Among its other types of case, those concerning the appointment and dismissal of civil servants bulk large.

Of various other administrative courts in existence, mention may be made of the National Insurance Tribunal (*Försäkringsdomstolen*), founded in 1961 to pass final judgement on appeals within the area indicated by its name, and the Tax Appeals Court (*Kammarrätten*),

[14] Cases concerning electoral registers, however, are finally decided by the relevant provincial government.

which dates back to 1618 and chiefly acts nowadays as a general tax appeals court—in some types of case, with the possibility of further appeal to the Supreme Administrative Court, in others not. It also functions as the administrative court of final instance on civil service pay and pensions questions.

In addition to administrative courts, administrative authorities may also hear appeals. Provincial governments may be cited as a case in point, and a good many boards (the Social Welfare Board, for instance) review on appeal decisions taken by local administrative agencies within their sphere of activity.

The device of the administrative appeal helps to secure uniformity of practice throughout the administrative system. This is sometimes regarded with a critical eye. "The hearing of administrative appeals", in the words of one legal commentator, "has . . . become one means among several of inducing administrative authorities to handle questions arising not according to their own view of what is objectively correct, but according to the government view of what is politically desirable."[15] Looked at from another angle, the administrative appeal permits a greater degree of decentralization than would otherwise be allowable. The fact that an administrative decision does not enter into legal effect until the expiry of the time for appeal may sometimes slow down business, but, on the other hand, it does help to guarantee respect for individual rights in cases where these are at risk.

[15] Sundberg, *op. cit.*, p. 302.

CHAPTER 7

External Controls on the Executive

THIS chapter attempts an assessment of the significance of six mechanisms for subjecting the executive to supervision from without. The most fundamental of the six is probably the publicity of official documents rule; the most celebrated—outside Sweden—the Ombudsmen; the most exotic, the reading of the minutes of the Council of State. These three in particular are complementary: the reading of the minutes of the Council represents one aspect of the publicity rule at work; the publicity rule assists the Ombudsmen in their operations; and the Ombudsmen help to maintain the publicity rule. The parliamentary auditors are included here by analogy with the financial select committees of the House of Commons.[1] The Advisory Council for Foreign Affairs is no very powerful control, but it is included because it is an interesting piece of democratic machinery. Interpellations and questions, though they are in Sweden rather a weak check, are growing slowly in importance.

THE PUBLICITY OF OFFICIAL DOCUMENTS

It is a general principle of Swedish administration that official documents, whether of state or local government authorities, shall be public. The rule is of long standing, having made its first appearance in a Freedom of the Press Act in 1766, been incorporated into another such Act in 1810, and finally reaffirmed in the latest Act of

[1] Their work has affinities with that of both the Public Accounts and Estimates Committees, but has been relatively small scale though it may expand in consequence of a recent reorganization. (See below, pp. 162–5.)

the series in 1949. It thus has the status of constitutional law. The principle is set down in these terms in the 1949 Act:

> To further free exchange of opinion and general enlightenment, every Swedish citizen shall have free access to official documents. . . . This right shall be subject only to such restrictions as are demanded out of consideration for the security of the realm and its relations with foreign powers, or in connexion with official activities for inspection, control or other supervision, or for the prevention and prosecution of crime, or to protect the legitimate economic interest of the state, communities and individuals, or out of consideration for the maintenance of privacy, security of the person, decency and morality.[2]

The operation of the rule in practice has, as might be expected, significant effects on Swedish administrative behaviour, though the differences from, say, the British pattern are not as great as might at first be thought.[3]

The right of access to official documents is open to everyone and not limited to parties affected.

> An official document that is not secret shall upon request and without cost be made available, immediately or as soon as possible, for examination by any person who desires to read and copy it at the place where it is kept, and such person shall further be entitled to obtain a copy of the document for a fixed fee. A document need not, however, be made available at the place where it is kept if that would meet with considerable difficulties.[4]

The civil servant in charge of a document is responsible for deciding in doubtful cases whether or not it is to be classified as public. If he decides that it cannot be produced, then the burden of proof lies on him.

The three Ombudsmen, amongst their other duties, keep an eye on the interpretation of the publicity rule in practice. One or two instances may be cited from the 1966 report of the Ombudsman for Civil Affairs. The first has a slight flavour of "Barchester Towers": a rural dean who appeared to be arguing that documents in his

[2] Tryckfrihetsförordningen (TFO) chapter 2, article 1.

[3] A good legal account of the rule is to be found in N. Herlitz, Publicity of official documents in Sweden, *Public Law*, London, 1958, pp. 50–69.

[4] TFO, chapter 2, article 8.

possession could not be made available on Saturday mornings because the office was shut is reminded that the law requires the rapid production of documents on request unless there are "considerable difficulties" in the way: the fact that the office was shut was not of itself a considerable difficulty, though by implication the clergyman would have been within his rights in claiming a delay till Monday on the grounds that he was writing his sermon and that the production of the documents would have involved him in a time-consuming search.[5] Again, disapproval is expressed of the refusal of a local government official to show a document to a newspaper editor, the refusal having been defended on the grounds that a question tabled in the local council on the subject-matter of the document had not yet been answered.[6] And a hospital consultant is taken to task for brusquely refusing to pass on to the appropriate hospital unit a legitimate request from a father for medical records in connection with his daughter's death.[7]

The Freedom of the Press Act gives a general indication of the nature of the exceptions to the publicity rule. Since 1937, the detailed regulation of these exceptions has been left to ordinary statute law—notably the 1937 Secrecy Act, with subsequent amendments. Thus, for example, a time limit of 70 years is in general set by the Secrecy Act before personal medical records can be inspected without the consent of the person concerned,[8] while a time limit of 20 years is prescribed before private income-tax returns can be similarly produced.[9] It would be tedious to list the exceptions laid down by the Act. Suffice it to say that they are numerous and hardly surprising. Small-scale adjustments are also made periodically by orders issued in pursuance of the Act.

The question of chief interest in the present context is the impact

[5] JO (Justitieombudsman—Ombudsman for Civil Affairs) report, 1966, pp. 357–63. Lutheran clergy are subject to the rule as members of the Established Church.

[6] *Ibid.*, pp. 364–7.

[7] *Ibid.*, pp. 367–70.

[8] Secrecy Act, article 14. The father in the case just mentioned had the right to inspect the documents concerning his daughter.

[9] *Ibid.*, article 17.

of the publicity rule on administrative practice. All items of business that are recorded in departmental or agency registers are open to public inspection unless they belong to one of the formally exempted categories. This has the effect of including virtually all communications coming in on remit from other public authorities, as well as other kinds of report and information from public bodies. It also includes a good many incoming communications from private persons (applications, appeals, etc.). Even private letters to civil servants are held to fall within the scope of the rule if they have a material influence upon an official decision. Some agencies make special arrangements for regular inspection by the Press of official documents received.

The publicity rule does not, however, do a great deal towards exposing the policy-making process to view—with the single admittedly large exception (noted in an earlier context) of the circulation of draft legislation, etc., on remit. In the first place, the Freedom of the Press Act allows the possibility of confidential documents in connection with the preparation of business:

> A memorandum or other note drawn by an authority solely to present or prepare a case or matter for decision shall not be deemed to be an official document in the hands of such authority unless, after the case or matter has been settled by the authority, the note is placed on permanent record.[10]

Secondly, it is quite in order for civil servants in a department or agency to stave off inquiries from the Press and others about a question currently under discussion by reference to the fact that a decision has not yet been reached. Thirdly, the minutes and other similar official records relating to a case or matter are in general required to be made available at the latest when the case or matter has been settled by the authority.[11] But it is not the practice to keep detailed minutes of the preliminary discussions; and again, although a civil servant introducing a piece of business is expected to minute any disagreement he may feel with the decision taken, in practice this seldom happens except in connection with civil service appointment

[10] TFO, chapter 2, article 4. [11] *Ibid.*, article 5.

cases.[12] Consequently the official records are usually rather bald, containing, for example, the names of the civil servant introducing and deciding the business, the names of those consulted, the nature of the decision reached, and, where appropriate, a brief statement of reasons. Fourthly, as was mentioned in an earlier context,[13] registration practice varies somewhat from one civil service agency to another, and it is sometimes possible for documents which should be subject to publicity to escape record. This question was raised in a couple of private member's motions in the 1957 Riksdag.[14] It is sufficient to reiterate here that this is a field for the vigilance of the Ombudsmen and that neglect to log appropriate records is, as one might expect, a culpable offence for a civil servant.

It will be evident from the above survey that there is considerable scope for variation in the extent to which different administrative agencies choose to lay bare the policy-making process. Oral communication in any case must escape review. On the whole it is probably true to say that more comes to light in the decentralized sectors of the administration than in the departments.

In conclusion, then, what is the practical significance of the publicity rule? The first, and one of the most important, effects has been discussed in a previous chapter[15] and so will merely be recorded here: the rule enables a considerable amount of informed debate to take place when draft legislation and commission reports are being circulated on remit between the various administrative authorities concerned. Divergences of view between these authorities are brought to light and an opportunity is given for facts that have been overlooked to be taken into consideration. At the same time the opposition parties are provided with a variety of material for use against the government in debate.

Secondly, the rule enables a private individual to enjoy guaranteed access to documents which enable him the more effectively to guard his rights *vis-à-vis* the administration. An individual who is a party

[12] Heckscher, *Svensk statsförvaltning i arbete*, pp. 153–4.
[13] See Chapter 3.
[14] FK 1957: 208 and AK 1957: 253.
[15] See Chapter 4.

in a dispute with the administration has a wider right of access to documents than that belonging to citizens in general. For example, an authority seeking to withhold a document from him on one of the specified legal grounds is expected to produce the document nevertheless unless there are especially important reasons why this should not be done.[16] The rule therefore has an impact in the field of administrative appeals.

Thirdly, the documents relating to the qualifications and conduct of civil servants are available for scrutiny in connection with applications for other posts, promotions, disciplinary measures, etc. So also are the documents relating to persons seeking entry into the public service. It has been noted earlier that divergences of view between those sitting on appointment boards and the like may find expression in the minutes. It is therefore possible, and it does sometimes happen, that an unsuccessful applicant for a post can make use of the documents to "complain himself into"[17] the desired position on appeal. In consequence of this he may find himself serving under an unsympathetic chief.

Such occasional awkwardnesses are, however, considered a small price to pay for the benefits of the publicity rule. It can act as a powerful protection for individual rights; it helps the Press to publicize what ought to be publicized—the fact that the rule is set out in successive Freedom of the Press Acts is no accident; it assists in producing a spirit of reasonableness and public service in the administration. The last word may appropriately be left to a Swedish commentator: "If the Swedish administration has . . . on the whole become less 'bureaucratic' recently than it was a century ago, the cause is probably . . . to be traced not so much to the bureaucrats becoming pleasanter nor to recruitment altering as to the significance of public criticism."[18] Public criticism is made chiefly through the Press, and the Press has the publicity rule as its ally.

[16] B. Wennergren, Förvaltningsförfarandet i ärenden angående enskilda, in Andrén (ed.) *et al.*, *Svensk statsförvaltning i omdaning*, Almqvist and Wiksell, Uppsala, 1965, pp. 70–71.

[17] The phrase is owed to Heckscher, *op. cit.*, pp. 177–8.

[18] Heckscher, *op. cit.*, pp. 196–7.

THE INSPECTION OF THE MINUTES OF THE COUNCIL

The availability of the minutes of the formal Council for inspection may be regarded as a special application of the rule that official documents shall be public. The Secrecy Act in fact lays down that most Council minutes shall not be available for scrutiny without government permission until 2 years from their date of issue. It also contains saving clauses to the effect that the Government may prescribe a longer period of secrecy for these minutes—up to 50 years—and that classified foreign policy and defence minutes are not to be released for 50 years without government permission.[19] The Instrument of Government requires that separate minutes shall be kept in secret foreign policy questions (article 9) and matters of military command (article 15), and later continues:

> It is incumbent on the Standing Committee on the Constitution to ask for the minutes kept by the Council of State. The separate minutes referred to in Article 9 may only be demanded, however, with reference to a particular matter specified by the Committee. In such case the King shall consider whether, in the light of the security of the realm or of other particularly important reasons determined by relations with foreign powers, he finds any objection to the delivery of the minutes of the Committee. They shall not be refused until the Advisory Council for Foreign Affairs has had an opportunity to express its views on the subject. Minutes relating to matters of military command may be demanded only with reference to matters generally known and specified by the Committee.[20]

The Standing Committee on the Constitution mentioned in this article is, it will be remembered, one of the Riksdag standing committees. It asks annually for the Council minutes *en bloc* for the previous parliamentary year (i.e. from the day of the opening of the previous Riksdag to the day of the opening of the current Riksdag). Later minutes may also be asked for if desired, and sometimes are; the special categories of secret minute named by the Instrument of Government are, of course, exempt from the general requisition. The Standing Committee on the Constitution—henceforth the

[19] Secrecy Act, article 1.

[20] RF, article 105.

SCC—is thus given a privileged position in respect of access to Council minutes, and the documents relating to the committee scrutiny of those minutes may not be made public before the expiry of the statutory 2-year secrecy period without committee approval.

The unreality of Council minutes in certain respects has been noted in an earlier context. The minutes consist of a number of substantial volumes arranged according to the various departments of State; and they record the items of business introduced into Council from each department, the advice which the Minister concerned is supposed to have given on each item to the King, and the decisions which are finally taken in the name of the King.

A somewhat curious procedure has traditionally been followed by the SCC when the minutes are being "considered". The committee splits up into four divisions for the purpose, each division concentrating on the minutes which relate to the business of two or three particular departments—though any foreign policy minutes are taken in plenary session. The rubric for each item of business is read out by the chairman in each case, and any member suspecting that the matter in question has been mishandled in some way may then ask for the rest of the minutes concerning it. If these appear to lend weight to his suspicions, then the item concerned is noted, and all the subsidiary documents connected with it are later requested in the name of the committee as a whole.[21] They are then handed over to the member who first raised the issue so that he may eventually report his findings. Final action is naturally left to the discretion of the committee, though criticisms of ministers may be embodied in minority reports. The formal assumption implicit in the constitutional rules is that evidence of any misdemeanour is invariably obtained from a reading of the minutes themselves. In fact, most of the points which are raised, are raised because they are matters of common knowledge which have been aired in the Press, or because they have been suggested to an MP by an interested outsider. Not much is to be extracted from the actual process of reading out rubrics.[22]

[21] The convention is that requests are always granted.

[22] O. von Zweigbergk, *Svensk politik, 1905–1929*, Bonniers, Stockholm, 1929, has a good chapter on this subject, pp. 208–18.

This raises the point that a good many of the matters ventilated by the committee, or by a minority within it, have already been discussed on earlier occasions—inevitably so, since the minutes received by the committee refer to the previous year. Consequently, the debates on the main committee report, which usually take place in April or May, often lack animation and, to some extent at least, are demonstrations of political shadow-boxing.

The scrutiny of the Council minutes was of course intended to be a scrutiny of the conduct of ministers as the King's advisers and the highest civil servants in the realm. It was designed to ensure that ministers were brought to account collectively or individually not only for the advice which they give but also for their illegal and injudicious actions. Ministerial responsibility is formally both a legal and a political responsibility. Indictable offences are indicated in outline in one of the articles of the Instrument of Government,[23] and they are enumerated in detail in a special law on the criminal responsibility of ministers:[24] they range from refusing to withhold countersignature to unconstitutional royal decisions to attempting a *coup d'état*. If the SCC finds evidence of any such violations, it shall order the Ombudsman to bring an action against the Minister or ministers concerned before a special Court of Impeachment. Political responsibility is drawn in very wide terms:

> Should the Standing Committee on the Constitution observe that the members of the Council of State collectively or one or more of them, in their advice upon public measures, have not paid due regard to the true welfare of the State, or that any Councillor of State has failed to perform his duties with impartiality, zeal, ability and energy, it shall bring the matter to the knowledge of the Riksdag, which, if it finds that the welfare of the realm so requires, may inform the King in writing of its desire that he remove from the Council of State and from office the person or persons criticized.[25]

All of these provisions have an archaic ring. Impeachment was last resorted to in 1854 and was never successful on any of the five occasions on which it was used: the Court of Impeachment was in

[23] RF, article 106.
[24] Ansvarighetslag för statsrådets ledamöter, 1810.
[25] RF, article 107.

fact so constituted as to be sympathetic to the King and his ministers, and it would be a highly improbable body to conduct criminal proceedings under present-day circumstances, containing as it does, for example, the commanders of the Stockholm Garrison and Naval Station and "the senior member of each of the administrative boards of the realm".[26] The political responsibility clause is drafted in terms appropriate to civil service responsibility of the normal Swedish type: "impartiality" is expected of members of the Council, and the phraseology makes it clear that judgement is primarily to be passed on their administrative skill. The incompatibility of the rules with the basic assumptions of a modern cabinet system is too obvious to be worth expounding.

It may well then be asked what purpose is still served by the reading of the Council minutes. The Riksdag has never in fact petitioned the King for the removal of a Minister under the political responsibility clause. The most that has happened is that the Lower House has on occasions minuted with approval a formal criticism of a Minister made in the annual report of the SCC. This occurred four times during the inter-war period, and on one (unique) occasion the censure implied was sufficiently strong to result in the resignation of the Minister involved (Wohlin, Minister of Finance, 1929). But this was during the minority government era, when the SCC could and did frequently make formal criticisms of ministers without being inhibited by the fact that such criticisms might carry a political barb (the number of criticisms in the annual committee report rose to a peak of 15 in 1922, when the record of two unpopular civil service ministries which had been in office in 1920–1 was under review). Formal criticisms have been very few and far between—five in all—in the post-war years of majority government. It is remarkable at first sight that there should have been any, but occasionally, for example, a Minister without Portfolio may be a target for criticism and occasionally the opposition parties may carry the day by lottery in an equally divided committee. One case of the latter kind arose in

[26] RF, article 102. The boards in question are, however, regarded as being limited to five of the more ancient foundations for the purposes of this article of the constitution.

1964 when the representatives of the opposition parties in the SCC banded together to table formal criticisms of the Ministers of Defence and of Foreign Affairs for allegedly failing to keep the spy Wennerström under close enough observation when he was working in these two departments. The committee was equally split and so the outcome had to be decided by lot—with the result that the criticism of the Defence Minister was defeated and appeared as a minority report, while that of the Foreign Minister was accepted, only to be voted down in the two Houses.[27] This, incidentally, was a classic case of a debate occurring in the Houses on the committee report in connection with a topic that had already been widely discussed months before in other contexts.

The chief interest of the annual debate on the stewardship of the Government as revealed by the Council minutes lies in the points made by the opposition parties on the SCC and in the informal criticisms of ministerial action which the committee is at times prepared to make without involving the constitutional responsibility clause. These latter, which have been running at an average rate of two or so a year over the last decade—the signs were, until 1967 at least, that they were becoming more common—are usually directed at minor irregularities of an administrative character. Some provide a parallel to the kind of criticism made by the Select Committee on Statutory Instruments in Britain—e.g. the 1956 report criticized the fact that thirty or so administrative orders had been brought into force before publication the previous year, and several other reports have pointed out similar transgressions. Among other practices subjected to adverse comment have been: failure to consult an administrative agency which should have been consulted at the draft stage of a Bill (1945); injudicious interpretation of the conditions attached to a parliamentary vote of supply (1946); insufficient supervision of the spare-time employment entered into by civil servants on administrative boards (1961); failure to consult the Advisory Council for Foreign Affairs on trade agreements (1962 and 1964); impairing the efficiency of provincial governors by asking them to take on too many extra tasks (1964); and improperly granting a

[27] SCC Memo. No. 21, 1964.

permit for a sizeable lottery in aid of the Social Democratic party and its Youth League (1966). This last item in the list raises the point that even the innocuous-seeming device of reporting "technical" items to the Riksdag without calling for action against the Minister concerned may have a political edge. Certainly the Social Democratic half of the SCC was stung into withdrawing support from all the half-dozen or so informal criticisms brought forward in 1966, so that these only got through by the luck of the draw (they were eventually simply minuted by the Houses)—and 1966 was the second year in succession in which allegedly technical objections to ministerial practice had produced lengthy and heated political controversies. The difficulty, of course, is to separate the political from the administrative: the mould in which the work of the SCC has to be cast inevitably makes this separation more difficult. The risk is that the minor but useful role which the SCC performs in supervising administrative practice is in danger of being vitiated by the political element. Its problem, therefore, would seem to be to develop a select-committee type of approach. As the Commission on the Constitution put it: "the scrutiny of and reporting on administrative practice should constitute the staple element in the supervision of the exercise of office by Councillors of State".[28] Ironically, the committee would probably function best if it returned in one sense to the original intention of the constitution makers of 1809—and approached ministers primarily as the highest civil servants in the realm.

It should be said in conclusion that in 1967 the SCC broke with precedent and made an evident effort to act in the spirit of the Commission's recommendations. Eschewing even the device of the informal criticism, it put forward ten unanimous comments on governmental procedures and on administrative practice. (Subjoined to these was a separate minority "opinion" signed by the Conservative and Liberal members of the committee expressing concern at the rate of increase of civil service establishments in the departments.) Ministers did not greet the new device with much enthusiasm—partly, it would seem, because it was unauthorized and irregular, and partly, too, perhaps, because of the content of one or

[28] SOU, 1963: 17, p. 454.

two of the new comments (e.g. a request to the Government to be more expeditious in the handling of official Riksdag messages). The difficulties in the way of achieving a select-committee type of relationship do, however, seem on the way to being resolved: the SCC in 1968 urged a reform along the lines recommended by the Commission, and the ministerial responsibility rules have just been rescinded as part of the 1968/9 constitutional reform.

THE PARLIAMENTARY AUDITORS

The twelve parliamentary auditors are required "to inspect the government, management and condition of the administration, the Bank of Sweden and the National Debt Office in accordance with the Instrument of Government and special instructions".[29] Their special instructions prescribe that they shall, "without, insofar as circumstances allow, overlooking details, chiefly review general dispositions, administration and results".[30] Attention to detail has become increasingly impossible as the scope of state activity has widened, so that the auditors have increasingly concentrated on questions of general interest and of wider economic significance. They have also, by convention, long been free to comment on administrative topics not strictly connected with financial administration. They are, however, required to carry out a standard audit of the accounts of the Bank of Sweden and the National Debt Office.

The parliamentary auditors are the nearest Swedish equivalent to the financial select committees of the House of Commons, but they have not been so strongly staffed and organized. Until 1968, six were elected from each House of the Riksdag for a year at a time, the elections being held in accordance with the proportional representation principle. Each party group by convention operated a seniority rule, choosing its longest-serving members for the vacancies. Re-election did not usually occur more than once or twice. Each member had a substitute who took over when he was unable to attend.

[29] Riksdag Act, article 72.

[30] Article 13, *Instrument for Parliamentary Auditors*. This is quoted from the rules valid until 1968. A new instrument is now being adopted as part of the reorganization of the auditors' work.

This organizational framework was not felt to be very satisfactory, and in 1967 a special inquiry into the subject reported in favour of an overhaul. A reform has now been put through based in large measure on the inquiry report—although the recommendation has not been accepted that the auditors should be reconstituted as a Parliamentary Audit and Accounts Committee working in sections with a secretariat equivalent in strength to that of a parliamentary joint standing committee. Instead, an SCC proposal has been adopted giving the auditors a status roughly equivalent to that of members of the board of the National Debt Office with a salary much above the old level. Under this new dispensation there will continue to be twelve auditors and twelve deputies elected as before by Parliament, but they will now serve for a 3-year term of office and the seniority rule will no longer apply.

The major task of the auditors is to search out evidence of wasteful expenditure and to make suggestions for economies. To this end they can travel about and hear witnesses freely. Their consolidated reports used, before 1968, to be delivered to the Riksdag in December each year—one report on the governmental sector of the administration, one on the Bank of Sweden, and one on the National Debt Office. The first of these reports contained thirty or forty items and was considered in Committee of Supply before being forwarded, with comments, to the Riksdag. The report arrived at an unfortunate time for the Committee of Supply, which found itself plunged more or less simultaneously into a scrutiny of the Government's finance plan for the forthcoming year. But it would be unfair to conclude that this was the reason why the Committee of Supply seldom had many qualifications to make to what the auditors had to say. The reports on the Bank of Sweden and the National Debt Office were delivered to the Committee on Banking for scrutiny and transmission to Parliament: they seldom raised more than a small number of points apiece, and they attracted less general interest than the report on the government sector of the administration. Under the revised regulations the auditors are empowered to report on questions as they arise and the old consolidated annual reports will disappear. The auditors will also be able to ask administrative agencies for their official views by circulating matters to them on remit, and they are now authorized to act with a greater degree of independence of Parliament, e.g. by suggesting reforms direct to the Government.

A few examples of the kind of item brought to the attention of the Riksdag in the auditors' reports may be of interest. The 1957 Riksdag was prompted by one report to ask that the division of functions between the departments of State be overhauled, and the government finance plan for 1963 recorded that this had been done and gave details. Also in 1957 the auditors called for an inquiry into the division of the country into provinces, recommending that the smaller provinces should disappear because they involved unduly high administrative costs and because office rationalization would be easier in large-scale units. This idea had already been very much in the air, having been vainly put forward in various forms in private members' motions in the Riksdag in 1945, 1953, and 1957. The Committee of Supply gave it partial acceptance, successfully recommending that a start be made by surveying the Stockholm and Gothenburg regions. A commission of inquiry on the larger topic was subsequently set up by the Government. Among other proposals made by the auditors may be mentioned a plan to save costs by concentrating all women prisoners in Sweden in one gaol in view of the decrease in their numbers since the extension of the system of supervision orders (1950 report); the desirability of rapidly disposing of properties in connection with shut-down railway lines (1964 report); the need for a costing survey of gravel and other unmetalled roads (also 1964); and the undesirability of making 1 per cent of the national income an absolutely rigid target for the level of aid to underdeveloped countries (1966).

The supervisory work of the parliamentary auditors is quite overshadowed in scale by that carried on within the administration itself. Nevertheless, the auditors are a useful if modest complement to the activities of the governmental sector in the financial field and they provide the Riksdag with a good deal of valuable information. They do not, of course, have any power to require the Government to comply with their suggestions for reform. By convention, however, they steer clear of party political controversies and their suggestions carry the greater weight as a result.

INTERPELLATIONS AND QUESTIONS

Interpellations in the Swedish Parliament have never acquired the formidable character of their French namesakes. They are traditionally a rather solemn kind of written question which is intended to lead to a debate. A brief debate often ensues, but it does not end in a vote expressing confidence or no confidence in the Government. The chief purpose of the interpellation, in fact, is to seek information from the Government or to criticize some aspect of its policy—much like an ordinary question in the House, but traditionally in connection with matters of greater political importance. The procedure is hence rather elaborate: the interpellation must be accompanied by a reasoned case in support and be approved by the appropriate House[31] before being forwarded via the Speaker to the Minister concerned. There is no obligation on the Minister to reply, but he almost always does so—not infrequently after an interval of about a month. The reply normally takes the form of a written memorandum prepared by the relevant department and circulated to the interpellator and other members of the House before being given orally in an abridged version by the Minister. No set hour or day of the week is fixed for these proceedings, which take place during the ordinary course of business at a time usually agreed upon between Minister, Speaker, and interpellator. The interpellator leads off, and subsequent debate—if any—is free and unrestricted.

Questions—of the traditional type—are also written and produce either oral answers or written answers along the same lines as the answers usually given to interpellations, but they require neither an accompanying reasoned supporting section nor House approval and they are not normally intended to lead to a debate.[32] It was ruled in

[31] Approval is a formality under all normal circumstances. Håstad, *op. cit.*, pp. 103–4.

[32] Questions, like interpellations, do not have to be answered but usually are—and more quickly than interpellations.

1949 that only the Minister and the questioner should normally speak to them (more than once if desired). Since, however, they may concern important and controversial topics, provision was at the same time made that a general debate could be opened on the subject-matter of a question if a member moved for this and the House approved. In 1967, largely in consequence of the rising number of questions, both houses adopted a rule that oral answers and discourses by questioners should be limited to 3 minutes apiece.

Interpellations and questions have indeed both been tending to increase in numbers of recent years. Interpellations in the early sixties averaged between 150 and 200 a year for the two Houses combined, questions averaged about or just under half that number until 1964, when they climbed sharply to 125 on what has proved to be a generally upward curve.[33] No very clear distinction can in fact be drawn between the two nowadays in respect of their subject-matter, as a few random samples drawn from the parliamentary records for 1964 will indicate.[34] In that year interpellations were asked about, *inter alia*: the position of housewives under national insurance; Swedish action in connection with South African apartheid policy; economic aid to handicapped students; and a 5-day week in schools. Questions were asked about: anti-unemployment measures in Norrbotten province; elk-hunting regulations; the use of the car-tax fund for speeding up road repairs; and the opportunities for schoolchildren on holiday to obtain paid employment. Again, in spring 1967, for example, we find both interpellations and questions being asked in connection with drug addiction in schools.

It is tempting to attribute the still comparatively small total of interpellations and questions to a clause in the Instrument of Government which was designed to prevent the Riksdag from prying too closely into matters properly belonging to the executive. The clause reads:

[33] Cf. the tables given in N. Andrén, *Modern Swedish Government*, pp. 93 and 94.

[34] The examples are taken at random from questions Nos. 26–36 in the Upper House and Interpellations Nos. 26–36 in the Lower.

> Matters relating to the appointment and removal of officials, the decisions, resolutions and judgements of the executive or judicial authorities, the affairs of private citizens or corporations, or the execution of any law, ordinance or regulation, shall in no case or manner be made subject to consideration or investigation by the Riksdag, its houses, or committees, except as literally prescribed by the fundamental laws.[35]

This rule originated in the separation of powers era and is also to be read against the background of the decentralized administrative system. The Commission on the Constitution wanted to sweep it away, apart from a safeguard for the affairs of private citizens or corporations. It seems unlikely, however, that the rule has any very crippling effect nowadays upon either interpellations or questions, although it has undoubtedly contributed to inhibiting them in earlier times. The position has been summarized thus in the Commission report:

> The interpretation which views the clause as a ban on any mention in parliamentary discussions of the matters cited in the regulation may be taken nowadays to be out of date. . . . In general it may be said that the rule is honoured whenever, for example, a specific decision of the government is proposed for debate as a subject in its own right, but on the other hand an M.P. is considered to be free e.g. to use the decision he wishes to criticize as an illustration in (a supporting) context, such as . . . in the statement of purpose attached to a (private member's) motion or to an interpellation.[36]

Questions continue to present a harder problem, but the ingenuity of the questioner has often been able to get round the difficulty. The comparative scarcity of parliamentary questions seems likely to depend as much or more nowadays on the vigorous use of private members' motions, the publicity of official documents, and the system of administrative appeals.

Attempts have been made in recent years to inaugurate a regular question time. A first move in the direction of this reform was made in January 1955, when an SCC delegation which had been visiting the Norwegian Storting and had been impressed by the "question hour" there successfully recommended that traditional-style questions be put all together and answered at the one time on Fridays.

[35] RF, article 90. [36] SOU, 1963: 17, p. 462.

The intention was that a maximum of 2 minutes be taken for each question and each answer, but in the event the three questions tabled at the first sitting took 20 minutes between them and the project languished. Then, early in 1964, the Prime Minister revived the notion, suggesting that questions be handed in on Wednesdays for answer on Thursdays and that question-time be characterized by rapid exchanges between questioners and ministers. A Speakers' Conference approved, and in April 1964 the first new-style question time was held. Questions were to be handed in on Fridays for answer on Tuesdays, the Government announcing on Mondays which questions were to be dealt with on the following day. A time limit of one hour was put on the proceedings, and these started in the Lower House one hour before the Upper so that ministers could appear in both. Fifteen questions were disposed of in the Lower House in 51 minutes at the first session and eight in the Upper in rather less time. The whole affair was given full publicity, with live broadcasting and television in attendance.

> Most replies were informative [one chronicle records] and only now and again were the debates [*sic*] blemished by polemics. Unlike question-time in the British Parliament, the atmosphere was of course sedate in the Chambers, without cries of approval or invective, and when the pleasure of novelty has worn off it is improbable that Swedish question-times will be any great public attraction.[37]

The indications were that the forecast would be accurate, with questions taking longer to ask and answer and public interest declining. The cut-and-thrust style of exchange has never been popular in the Riksdag,[38] which has always prided itself on being a body for the transaction of public business and no frills. Nevertheless, the new procedures seem to have given a stimulus to the use of the parliamentary question: the extension of question time to other weekdays

[37] Report in *Nordisk kontakt*, **8** (1964) p. 500.

[38] Nor outside it, to judge from election campaigns and from the abortive attempt to start a Hyde Park Corner in Stockholm in the 1950's. On the style of parliamentary debate in Sweden, see Andrén, *op. cit.*, p. 95. For an account of a Swedish election, see N. C. M. Elder, The Swedish election of 1956, *Political Studies*, February 1957, pp. 65–78.

besides Tuesdays was mooted in 1965, and the opposition parties have recently taken more to using questions and interpellations as part of their general campaign against government policies. The stricter time limits for debating questions which were introduced in 1967 (as mentioned briefly above) seem likely, in conjunction with this development, to vitalize this particular control device still further.

THE ADVISORY COUNCIL FOR FOREIGN AFFAIRS

Reference has been briefly made already[39] to the Advisory Council for Foreign Affairs, and the role of the Riksdag in foreign policy has been charted elsewhere,[40] so that only a few notes on essentials will be offered here.

The Advisory Council for Foreign Affairs (henceforth ACFA) meets under the chairmanship of the King, as mentioned earlier, and has a membership of sixteen, drawn equally from each House according to the principle of proportional representation. The leaders of all the main opposition parties are to be found on it, virtually though not formally *ex officio*: the Communist Left are not numerous enough for representation (they had eight members in the Lower House after the 1964 elections and two in the Upper). Deputy members are elected at the same time, to the same number, and according to the same principles as full members: they can attend every meeting of the Council, whether or not any of the full members are present.

The function of the ACFA is to act as a parliamentary delegation which the Government is expected to consult at the formative stages of *all* major questions of foreign policy. It should thus be taken into government confidence about important matters which are not going to be laid before the Riksdag as a whole. In particular:

[39] Chapter 2, pp. 33–34.

[40] There is a good account in Andrén, *op. cit.*, pp. 143–8. See also Elder, *op. cit.*

> Should an occasion arise when the interests of the realm require that an agreement, which is of great importance but does not deal with a matter which the Riksdag is entitled to decide, be concluded without the confirmation of the Riksdag, this may be done, but in such a case the Council for Foreign Affairs, or the Foreign Affairs Committee, shall be given an opportunity to express its opinion before the agreement is concluded.[41]

The ACFA as mentioned earlier, has the same membership as the Foreign Affairs committee. The matters "which the Riksdag is entitled to decide" are financial agreements and agreements involving the use of the legislative power.

The intention is that the ACFA shall be given all the information required to give a useful opinion on the questions referred to it. "All available documents and information"[42] are to be submitted to it when it is consulted, and it is to be kept *au fait* with the general course of developments abroad: "At the beginning of each session of the Riksdag, and afterwards as often as circumstances may require, the Minister for Foreign Affairs shall present to the Advisory Council an account of such general aspects of the foreign policy situation as may become of importance for the realm."[42] The Council can be summoned at any time of year, irrespective of whether Parliament is in recess or dissolved; and any six of its members may have it convened by notifying the Minister for Foreign Affairs that they wish it to be consulted about a particular question.[43]

In return for these entitlements the members of the Council are required, on first attendance, to give an assurance that they will faithfully observe secrecy when the Government demands it. They are also bound to "observe the utmost caution with regard to communicating to others information concerning what occurs at meetings of the Council".[42]

No doubt consultation with the Council is made easier for the Government by the fact that all four major parties in Sweden share a basic unity of view about foreign policy questions and, in particular, all support the time-honoured neutralist line in international affairs. The record of consultation appears on the whole to be good, as far as the evidence goes. During the war-time years there was not

[41] RF, article 54. [42] *Ibid.* [43] RO, article 49.

much need to use the Council—a national coalition government was then in power—but even so it was heard in connection with some crucial matters, such as the German request for troop transit facilities and the Allied request that the export of ball-bearings to Germany be stopped. It does not seem to have been consulted until late in the day, however, on the Swedish mediation at the end of the second Russo-Finnish war. In the post-war years it seems generally to have been heard on the major issues—e.g. the decision to accept Marshall Aid and the abortive 1948–9 discussions for a Scandinavian pact based on mutual assistance outside NATO. It was not, on the other hand, consulted at an early stage of the negotiations on the much-disputed 1946 Trade and Credit Agreement with the USSR. More recently, it appears to be consulted about issues of concern to Sweden arising on the UN front—where, as in other international organizations (e.g. the Nordic Council), representatives of all four major parties are commonly to be found taking part in the Swedish delegations.

A change in the composition of the ACFA appears likely to come about as part of the set of constitutional reform proposals agreed between the parties for presentation to the 1968 Riksdag. The total number of members will be reduced to nine (with an equal number of deputy members) and the union between the ACFA and the Foreign Affairs Committee is scheduled for dissolution.

THE OMBUDSMEN

So much has been written, and heard, in English about Ombudsmen that the use of the original term may be allowed, despite the arrival of the Parliamentary Commissioner on the British scene.[44]

[44] Among the more useful literature on this topic may be mentioned articles by two Ombudsmen and by U. Lundvik in *The Ombudsman, Citizen's Defender* (ed. D. C. Rowat), London, Allen & Unwin, 1965, pp. 22–57; B. Chapman, *The Profession of Government*, Allen & Unwin, London, 1959, chapter 12; and *The Citizen and the Administration* (the Whyatt Report), Stevens, London, 1961, chapter 10. Background information will be found *in extenso* in N. Alexanderson, Justitieombudsmannen, Militieombudsmannen, Tryckfrihetskommittén, *Sveriges Riksdag*, vol. 16, Petterson, Stockholm, 1935.

In any case, the two offices are dissimilar enough to warrant different names. The chief purpose of this account will be to bring out some of the major points about the Swedish institution and to illustrate them where appropriate with reference to some concrete examples.

Until 1966 there was a strict constitutional division of labour in Sweden between two Ombudsmen, one being charged with the supervision of the civil and the other of the military sector of the administration. This division has now been taken out of the basic laws. The aim and effect of the change is to make it easier for the work load to be equitably divided—and for more Ombudsmen to be created at need. This enables the Ombudsman concerned with the military sector to carry on, in fact if not in name, and to continue operating in his old familiar jurisdiction while relieving the heavier pressure on the civil affairs specialist. In 1967 the Riksdag has in fact decided that there shall now be three of these officials and that they shall for the time being divide up the work load between themselves according to several broad areas of specialization (defence, welfare, etc.). A brief account of the background to these changes is given at the end of this survey.

The Ombudsmen have to be expert in the law. The Instrument of Government, as now amended, prescribes: "The Riksdag shall appoint at least two citizens of known legal ability and outstanding integrity... to supervise the observance of laws and ordinances...."[45] It is a part, though rather an incidental part, of their duties to comment on the practical operation of laws and ordinances. They have also to scrutinize the conduct and working of judges and courts—a function which may be left out of account in the present context, even though it absorbs a good deal of their time and energy. Again, and probably most important of all these days, they have to watch over the operations both of military personnel and of civil servants at state and local level and "to institute proceedings before the competent courts against those who, in the execution of their official duties, have through partiality, favouritism or other cause committed any unlawful act or neglected to perform their official duties properly".[45] The wide responsibility of public servants in

[45] RF, article 96.

Sweden for faults committed in the course of duty has been noted in an earlier context:[46] the field of surveillance of the Ombudsmen has to be drawn correspondingly wide.

Legal knowledge is clearly indispensable for these duties, and in fact it is the convention that Parliament chooses men qualified to act as judges to perform them. The choice of officials is formally made by the vote of a special electoral college consisting of forty-eight MPs drawn equally from both Houses and themselves elected on a proportional representation basis. In fact the matter is usually settled in advance by agreement between the party groups concerned. Election is for a 4-year term, and re-election is permissible. The convention which in fact obtains has been succinctly put by Håstad: "The Riksdag dislikes the office changing hands too frequently, but neither does it want Procurators[47] to hold their position for life: a ten to twelve year period is regarded as being about the optimum for effective supervision of the administration."[48]

The jurisdiction of the original Ombudsman for Civil Affairs was so drawn as to exclude from surveillance the members of the Council of State. This is natural enough: the members of the Council of State were, as has been shown, made subject to the scrutiny of the SCC under the arrangements of 1809. The Ombudsman for Civil Affairs, whose office was created at the same time, was, however, given the task of taking charge of the prosecution of ministers before the Court of Impeachment at the instance of the SCC.[49] The Ombudsman for Military Affairs was a much more recent phenomenon, having been created in 1915 primarily to look after the interests of conscripts shortly after the introduction of compulsory long-term national service. His function was thus, as the name indicates, to carry out supervisory duties similar in nature to those of his colleague in respect of persons paid out of the armed services vote

[46] Chapter 6, pp. 139–41.

[47] "Riksdag Procurators" is a term in earlier currency, found in the official translation of the Swedish Constitution referred to earlier. It is discarded in the present text because it has not won its way into English usage.

[48] E. Håstad, *The Parliament of Sweden*, p. 135.

[49] RF, article 106.

(i.e. including members of the armed forces and also civil servants working in defence administration).

It has been mentioned in an earlier context[50] that the competence of the Ombudsman for Civil Affairs was drawn to include the investigation of complaints against the clergy of the Established (Lutheran) Church.[51] Local government officials, and members of local government administrative bodies acting as agents of the central administration, were to some extent brought within his jurisdiction in 1957.[52] The chief purpose of this reform was to enable him to supervise a whole new range of cases involving the deprivation of individual freedom by administrative action—e.g. compulsory committals to local authority mental hospitals and to local authority institutions for alcoholics.[53] As early as 1949 the First Committee on Laws—the parliamentary standing committee which considers the annual reports of the Ombudsmen—had pointed out the irrationality of the supervision arrangements then existing: "There would . . . appear to be no good reason why a person who has been deprived of his liberty by being admitted to a local authority mental hospital should be worse off in this respect than he who has been taken into a state institution."[54] The widening of the powers of the Ombudsman was, however, accompanied by deliberate safeguards for the independence of local self-governing authorities. Members of provincial and local councils were made exempt from supervision by the insertion of a clause limiting the Ombudsman to overseeing "those subject to full responsibility for their official conduct."[55] Local councillors are not subject to full responsibility, being only punishable as public servants for corruption and breach of secrecy, and for these offences any public prosecutor is fully competent to start an action.[56] The Ombudsman

[50] See above, on the publicity of official documents.

[51] See above, p. 154, n. 5.

[52] Government Bill, 1956: 161.

[53] A full discussion of the types of case involved is to be found in the report of the inquiry preceding the reform, SOU, 1955: 50, pp. 63–98.

[54] First Committee on Laws report, 1949: 15, quoted from SOU, 1955: 50, p. 63.

[55] RF, article 96, as amended 1957.

[56] H. Strömberg, *Allmän förvaltningsrätt*, Gleerup, Lund, 1962, p. 64.

was at the same time enjoined not to intervene wherever there was the possibility of lodging an administrative appeal.

The individual responsibility of public officials in Sweden for offences committed in the course of duty thus constitutes one ground for the importance of the Ombudsmen in the Swedish system of government. Another, less important, factor working to the same end is the circumstance that, if a private individual feels himself to have suffered damage from an offence committed by a higher civil servant[57] in the course of duty, he can only launch a prosecution with the concurrence of an official prosecutor. His natural allies here are the Ombudsmen. Such cases are, however, rare: it is the host of lesser grievances against civil servants of whatever rank which weigh more heavily and which have earned the Ombudsmen their reputation as "tribunes of the people". The irony is that at first the Ombudsmen were not primarily intended to discharge this function—or rather, the Ombudsman for Civil Affairs was not. He was intended to be a parliamentary servant whose main task would be

> to keep a watchful eye on the government so that it did not misuse its authority to prompt subordinate officials to illegalities and transgressions. . . . [His] action would certainly appear in such cases to be outwardly directed against the relevant civil servant but in reality [it would be directed against] the government which was considered to have inspired the breach of law.[58]

The heavy weapon of prosecution is only used in a small minority of cases. The 1965 report of the Ombudsman for Civil Affairs, for example, records that two cases were sent for trial out of a net total of 1407 items of business,[59] while the 1966 report records three

[57] Definable in this context as a civil servant against whom an action properly lies in the Supreme Court or in one of the higher courts (*hovrätter*).

[58] SOU, 1955: 50, pp. 54–55.

[59] JO (Ombudsman for Civil Affairs—Justitieombudsman) report, 1965, p. 11. The net total is arrived at by the subtraction from the gross total of cases referred elsewhere, of reports on remit, and of cases pending for various stated reasons. It should, incidentally, be added that since all three Ombudsmen are to be called justitieombudsman henceforth, the force of the old abbreviation 'JO' will soon be weakened.

cases out of a net total of 1542 items.[60] Each report is divided into a section on the judiciary and a section on the administration. The 1965 and 1966 reports between them give the case history of three prosecutions initiated by the Ombudsman in the administrative sector at earlier dates. Space does not allow any exhaustive treatment, but a brief note about a couple of these prosecutions may be of interest.

The Deputy Director-General and a Chief Engineer of the Civil Aviation Board were indicted in 1962 and convicted in 1963 of dereliction of duty in connection with a private airline flight. The airline in question had issued invitations to some seventy people to take part in a "Christmas shopping flight" to Paris and back in December 1961. The chief engineer and his wife were among those who received invitations, and they took part, after the permission of the Deputy Director-General of the Civil Aviation Board had been asked for and granted. At the time the invitation was received the chief engineer was concerned in the consideration of "very important permit questions of a non-routine character"[61] in connection with precisely the same airline that had made the offer. The prosecution did not allege that the acceptance of the benefit could be suspected of influencing the engineer in the course of his duty, but they did maintain that it was calculated, in all the circumstances, to give rise to doubts in the public mind as to his impartiality and that it was likely to damage public confidence in his exercise of office. The Deputy Director-General was indicted for giving the engineer permission to go on the flight. Both he and the engineer were fined.[62]

The second case involving prosecution of civil servants concerned a Provincial Governor, a Provincial Secretary (the Governor's chief official), and a Provincial Police Superintendent. The prosecution was initiated in 1963, the case heard in 1964 and again, on appeal, in 1965. It concerned failure to take the necessary action on government instructions concerning contingency defence planning for police forces. These instructions had been contained in a secret

[60] JO report 1966, p. 11.
[61] *Ibid.*, p. 265.
[62] JO report 1965, pp. 261–77.

directive sent out to provincial governments in 1951. The Ombudsman had addressed a message to the provincial government in question in 1956 calling upon it to fulfil its duties in accordance with the directive. In 1962 he discovered in the course of a tour of inspection that the required action had still not been taken. The prosecution ensued. The Provincial Secretary and the Provincial Police Superintendent were convicted of dereliction of duty and fined in the court of first instance, but the Provincial Governor was acquitted. The Ombudsman thereupon appealed to the Supreme Court in respect of the Provincial Governor and won his case, with the result that the Provincial Governor also was fined. The two other functionaries, who had appealed against their convictions, lost their appeals.[63]

The great majority of items of business handled by the Ombudsmen do not require any drastic interventions of this kind. The instruction which governs their operations in somewhat greater detail than the Constitution—it is, of course, issued by Parliament as their employer—envisages that cases of carelessness may be closed once the mistake has been rectified or an explanation given,[64] and the Ombudsmen have in practice interpreted this broadly to cover also deliberate misdemeanours of a less serious nature. Thus the 1965 report of the Ombudsman for Civil Affairs[65] records that no fewer than 722 items were written off (out of a gross total of 1864) "after hearing the relevant person or (after) other types of inquiry", while a further 283 items led to rectification or official comment or caution. A considerable number (381) were written off forthwith without any action being required:[66] the Ombudsmen customarily reply in such cases, however, giving reasons for not taking action, even though the complaints may have been somewhat crankish. In the 1966 report, 667 items (out of a gross total of 1859) are recorded as having been written off after inquiry; 400 led to rectification, official comment, or caution, and 453 were scrapped.[67]

[63] *Ibid.*, pp. 294–306.

[64] Instruction for the Riksdag's Ombudsmen, para. 4.

[65] The figures given in the text refer to the reports of this official. The work of the former Ombudsman for Military Affairs is considered briefly below, p. 184.

[66] JO report 1965, p. 11.

[67] JO report 1966, p. 11.

Complaints may be made against any public servant in the categories mentioned earlier by any member of the public writing direct to the Ombudsman. The complaints must be written and supported as far as possible with documentation and proof. The great majority of matters investigated originate in this way—in 1964, for example, there were 1239 such complaints, and in 1965 there were 1217. In a few cases the Ombudsman takes up questions on his own initiative on the basis of articles in the Press (eleven such instances are recorded in the 1965 report and eight in that for 1966). Not many items of business fall into this category, but some of them are important. The airlines prosecution referred to above, for example, is a case in point: it was on the basis of a Press report that the Ombudsman requested the Public Prosecutor in Stockholm to carry out a preliminary investigation, whereafter matters took the course outlined above. A good many pieces of business, too, originate as a result of the tours of inspection which the Ombudsman carries out—179 such items were notified in the 1965 report, 182 a year later. The usual procedure followed in the matter of inspections is that the Ombudsman concentrates on a different province each year, giving short notice of his arrival and looks through the files of a considerable number of authorities on the spot. Here again, as one holder of the office records,[68] Press reports may have a considerable influence on the pattern of his investigations.

The publicity given to the proceedings of the Ombudsman is a powerful aid to their efficiency. A Press representative calls each day to inspect the files and inward and outward correspondence, and Press reports often appear in consequence. On the whole the tendency is not to publicize the names of the civil servants concerned but even so, the widespread circulation given to so many items of business strengthens the authority of the Ombudsman *vis-à-vis* the administration.[69]

The Ombudsmen are granted access by the Constitution to all the information they may require in the course of their investigations,

[68] A. Bexelius, The Ombudsman for Civil Affairs, in Rowat, *op. cit.*, p. 29.

[69] For further information on this topic see Lundvik's article in Rowat, *op. cit.*, and also the Whyatt Report, para. 100.

including secret documents. The relevant clause gives them this power implicitly rather than explicitly: they

> may, whenever they consider it necessary in the exercise of their duties, attend the deliberations and decisions of . . . the administrative boards or the institutions established in their place . . . but shall have no right to express their views on such occasions; they shall also have access to the minutes and records of all courts, administrative boards and public offices. The King's officials in general are bound to afford [them] lawful assistance.[70]

These rules are interpreted broadly in practice to give them access to all relevant material, whether classified or not.[71]

Some illustrations, taken from the 1965 and 1966 reports of the Ombudsman for Civil Affairs, will now be offered to demonstrate a few leading types of case (examples connected with the working of the publicity of official documents principle have been quoted earlier and will not now be taken into account). It may be said by way of foreword that the cases selected for publication in the annual reports are in general clearly designed to serve for the guidance of administrators; a copy of each report is, in fact, sent out on publication to all civil servants who are likely to benefit.

Cases involving the failure of administrative authorities to give proper reasons for their decisions have been hardy perennials. In 1960, indeed, the Ombudsman asked the Government to issue a general order giving effect to the principle that departments, boards, etc., should state the reasons for decisions. Instances of the fault recurring are to be found in both the 1965 and 1966 reports. One authority, in rejecting an application from a small farmer for the purchase of some woodlands, simply referred him to paragraphs 3 and 4 in the relevant Act. The Ombudsman commented: "It could not be expected that the generality of applicants would have access to the legal text. . . . It should further be noted that paragraphs 3 and 4 in the Act contain a variety of reasons for rejection, wherefore reference to these clauses would not reveal the grounds on which the board had based its judgement."[72] Another authority in the same

[70] RF, article 9.

[71] Bexelius, *op. cit.*, p. 25.

[72] JO report 1965, p. 306.

sector of the administration reversed the decision of a lower instance in a land acquisition case without giving reasons. This provoked the Ombudsman to comment on the special importance of appellate bodies explaining the grounds for their decisions—so as to give subordinate authorities guidance and as a result to help ensure consistency of practice.[73]

Another type of case which frequently arises concerns the failure of administrative bodies to allow parties affected by a decision the opportunity to appear and give relevant information before the decision is taken. This again is a subject on which the Ombudsman has addressed a memorandum to the Government—in 1961, in this instance.[74] The importance of "the question of communication" (*kommuniceringsfrågan*), as it is customarily called, is particularly stressed in cases involving the imposition of a duty or the removal of a privilege. The issue has also arisen quite often in connection with applications to expand farms by the purchase of neighbouring land: the same Agricultural Executive Committee which had referred the small farmer to the law text is told that it should have given him the chance to state his case orally before it reached the decision to reject his application. The relevant statute implies the necessity of a proper investigation of applications; a proper investigation must be particularly thorough in the minority of cases where it is proposed to reject an application; and the chances are that the unpopularity which is the especial lot of agricultural executive committees would be lessened if applicants were afforded the opportunity to explain their position before their suit is decided.[75] Again, a case is cited in the 1966 report of the police neglecting to hear a taxi-driver before deciding to withdraw his cabby's licence—and the case is explicitly stated to be representative of many.[76]

It has been mentioned earlier, in connection with the extension of the Ombudsman's field of surveillance in 1957, that cases involving the deprivation of liberty by administrative action fall to his lot. They are, indeed, a particular concern of his. Thus, for example, a Finnish alcoholic who had attacked his unfaithful wife on various

[73] JO report 1965, pp. 302–5.

[74] JO report 1962, pp. 339 ff.

[75] *Ibid.*, pp. 306–15.

[76] JO report 1966, pp. 606–8.

occasions and who was adjudged to be a menace to public safety, was found to have been wrongly detained in a mental hospital for 7 months instead of having been committed to an alcoholics' institution where a shorter period of detention could reasonably have been expected.[77] The examining doctor in the case had certified the man on the grounds of a mental abnormality requiring detention, in line with a general tendency to refer more and more cases of alcoholism for mental hospital treatment—but this did not meet the requirements of the relevant statute, which requested proof of mental illness (e.g. alcoholic paranoia). The Ombudsman concluded:

> Equity strongly demands, in my opinion, that compensation be paid out of public funds on the grounds that L. has been wrongly deprived of his liberty because of the error which has been pointed out. At the very beginning of his stay in the mental hospital L. seems to have attempted to gain redress and discharge from the hospital through the agency of outsiders. . . . In support of this application for the payment of moneys out of public funds to L. I would cite Your Majesty's practice in dealing with similar applications from the Ombudsmen, the earliest [of them dating] from the 1820's.[78]

The frequent use by one provincial government of policemen to issue summonses to interviews in connection with (*inter alia*) child care cases is another administrative practice that has met with the Ombudsman's disapproval. The law requires that postal communication shall be used unless there is good reason to the contrary; an inquiry into the circumstances is therefore necessary before it is decided not to use the post; this had not generally been done by the authority under review. The use of police had been defended on the grounds that it ruled out any possibility of postal delay damaging the course of business, but this was insufficient reason. The practice was reprehensible because it added to the existing burdens on the police and because it could be unpleasant for the individuals affected. The criticism was designed (successfully) to bring procedure in the provincial government concerned more closely into line with that being followed elsewhere in the land.[79]

[77] *Ibid.*, pp. 519–29. [78] *Ibid.*, pp. 518–19.
[79] JO report 1965, pp. 382–96.

In all of the cases mentioned so far—except, of course, those ending in prosecution—the Ombudsman was content to end his review either with a simple recommendation that practice be altered or compensation paid or with a note that measures had been taken to meet his criticisms: in no case was the error sufficiently culpable to warrant anything more. Occasionally, however, a caution is given or, more rarely, the matter is referred to the superiors of the civil servant concerned for disciplinary action. A provincial official was, for example, given a caution as a result of a check on the security arrangements in respect of secret defence documents—a matter recorded in the 1965 report[80] but noticed in the course of a tour of inspection of a provincial government in 1962. The regulations required strict precautions to be taken in connection with the keys to the strongrooms, etc., where these secret documents must be kept. In this instance it was observed, amongst other things, that the duplicate key to the cupboard where the most important documents were preserved was itself kept in an office cupboard to which no fewer than five civil servants had a key.

The inspection of provincial governments has brought with it the right to criticize and influence practice in the issuing of local bylaws, since local bylaws are subject to provincial government ratification. Some curious examples of such bylaws were criticized in the 1965 report (they have had parallels in British experience): a ban on the consumption of alcoholic beverages in public places except in connection with licensed retailing; a ban on the playing of cards "or other comparable games" in public places; a requirement that dog-owners should not permit their dogs to foul the pavements ("only the more flagrant cases would be proceeded against" said the local government authority concerned).[81]

In the supervision of bylaws, however, the Ombudsman is merely reinforcing the work of the courts. The last illustration to be given in this short series raises more complex and important issues. A local government council for a time took no action to put things right after a ruling of the Supreme Administrative Court had invalidated as *ultra vires* a decision reached by the council to buy an hotel to

[80] JO report 1965, pp. 401–5.

[81] JO report 1966, p. 562.

cater for the tourist traffic. The purchase had already been effected while an appeal was pending against the decision to buy: the local authority had banked on the appeal failing, but in fact it succeeded. The Ombudsman, after studying the case, pointed out the existence of a gap in the statutes, because

> present law does not authorize a State authority to compel a commune to undertake measures to undo the execution of a decision nullified as unlawful. The absence of a legal remedy would appear to be explained historically by the fact that it was not considered necessary to reckon with the possibility that a commune would fail to respect the invalidation of a commune decision by an appellate authority.[82]

Cases of this kind of contumacy were, however, beginning to appear. The Ombudsman therefore suggested to the Government[83] that the possibility be investigated of empowering provincial governments to order communes, under penalty of a fine, to investigate when appropriate the feasibility of undoing the effects of annulled decisions. It should be added that the Ombudsman had got the case in the first instance because of an inquiry from a prominent administrative lawyer about (a) the culpability of local government *officials* in respect of the execution of a council decision liable to be reversed on appeal, and (b) the possible duty of the provincial government concerned to induce the commune to restore the *status quo*.[84] The case, here reduced to the barest essentials, points to the complexity of the legal questions with which the Ombudsman has at times to deal. It was not viewed by him as "an intervention in local self-government"[85] but rather as an attempt to right an illegality. He included, indeed, in his communication to the government a carefully reasoned plea for the widening of local authority powers in respect of tourism, etc., partly in order to diminish the risks of future legal *contretemps* in this field.

These examples of the Ombudsman in action will serve to indicate the range of the office. Many others could be adduced to show how he defends individual liberties, helps to improve administrative practice, watches over the operation of laws and ordinances and at

[82] *Ibid.*, p. 502. [83] *Ibid.*, pp. 498–505.
[84] *Ibid.*, pp. 307–45. No such duty was discoverable. [85] *Ibid.*, p. 503.

times acts in some respects like a Council on Tribunals. It is not surprising to find that he has, since 1941, been granted the salary of a Supreme Court judge. He has, too, a deputy, who is elected at the same time and in the same way and who must have the same qualifications.[86] The deputy takes over when the Ombudsman goes on holiday and also in the event of illness; he assists in making inspections, carrying out each year in some designated province a somewhat less extensive sampling analysis than his senior partner; and he has delegated items of business to deal with at stated intervals throughout the year, thus relieving the Ombudsman of some of the heavy pressure.

The Ombudsman for Military Affairs, even before the latest reform, enjoyed a similar salary and status to his colleague and was similarly assisted by a deputy. Far fewer complaints come in from individuals in this sector—usually they number less than a tenth of those received in the civil sector—but, on the other hand, three or four times as many matters tend to come up in the course of tours of inspection. Complaints of assault or insulting behaviour provide one recurrent type of business; among others may be mentioned negligence in respect of classified documents, use of military subordinates for non-official duties, sub-standard conditions of service, the payment of compensation for damage done on manœuvres, and the negligence of military medical staff in respect of patients.[87]

Agitation for the relief of the considerable and mounting workload of the Ombudsman for Civil Affairs made itself increasingly apparent in the Riksdag from the early 1950's onwards. Suggestions that his office be divided were tabled in private members' motions, for example, and rejected by the relevant parliamentary committees in 1954 and 1956 with the, in the circumstances, rather curious argument that the personal touch should be preserved as long as possible.[88] The inquiry which reported in 1955 on the general posi-

[86] RF, article 97.

[87] A more extended account of the office is given at first-hand by H. Henkow, in Rowat, *op. cit.*, pp. 51–57.

[88] Reports of Composite SCC and First Committee on Laws, 1954, No. 1, and similar committee 1956, No. 2.

tion of the institution similarly rejected the idea that business might be transferred from the Ombudsman for Civil Affairs to the Ombudsman for Military Affairs (whose burden was not so heavy).[89] For the moment all that was done was to allow the deputies to take over more work by delegation. The subject continued to engage the attention of MPs, however, and in 1963 no fewer than eight private members' motions in the field were referred to committee.[90] Among the schemes put forward was one for the splitting of the office in the civil sector between a specialist in judicial and another in administrative matters. Another plan envisaged the provision of one post which might be held by an indefinite number of persons—rather like the British Secretaryship of State. In the event the Government acted on a recommendation of the Commission on the Constitution that provision be made for "at least two" of these officials and that the division of labour be not specified in the basic laws.[91] The constitutional amendment required was tabled in 1964 and passed the following year.

The existence of the highly developed system of administrative appeals in Sweden has helped to restrict the number of Ombudsmen required to two for many years. The road has now been cleared towards a multiplication of the office and a third Ombudsman was created in 1968. No one could say that this is an instance of Parkinson's law at work.

[89] SOU, 1955: 50, pp. 132–3.

[90] Report No. 1 of Composite SCC—Committee on Banking—First Committee on Laws, 1963.

[91] SOU, 1963: 17, pp. 466–7.

EPILOGUE

Political Style and Political Change in Sweden with a Note on Provincial Government Reform

A GOOD deal has been said at various places in this book about the changes that have been taking place, or that are taking place, or that are in prospect, in the field of Swedish government. The theme has been recurrent, and it is perhaps appropriate to end this survey by taking a closer look at two characteristics of the Swedish political style that are significant in this connection and that have been mentioned in passing earlier in this book. The first of these characteristics is the spirit of *saklighet* or "matter-of-factness"; the second, the radical rationalist spirit that can be seen at work upon the task of reshaping the country's political institutions. This latter phenomenon in particular may finally be illustrated by a brief survey of the ferment of ideas that are in circulation in the field of provincial government reform.

The spirit of *saklighet* rates highly a cool, objective and dispassionate approach to questions of public policy. It antedates the era of modern parliamentary government—to be more specific, it was much more in evidence in nineteenth-century Sweden than in the eighteenth-century Sweden of the struggles between the Hats and the Caps and of the periods of royal absolutism. It can be seen, for example, in the political reflections of Louis de Geer, the originator of the nineteenth-century cameral reform. Here, as elsewhere, two strands may be detected: firstly, an essentially conservative belief that the national interest is best served by co-operation across factional barriers in a spirit of national unity; and, secondly an essentially liberal faith in the capacity of unemotional reasoned argument to winnow out the best possible solution to any given problem and so to bring about a steady and continuous progress in human affairs. This spirit, clearly, is congenial to what might be called the classical administrative cast of mind. It is not therefore surprising that it should have been current at a time when the bureaucracy were much engaged in political life—and when ministers were officially the highest civil servants in the realm. Again, the constitution of 1809, as we have seen, established a dualism between Government and Parliament. Since the Riksdag took itself seriously as an independent force, and since, moreover, it contained a large bureaucratic element, the circumstances were favourable for the spirit of *saklighet* to exert an influence on the political arena.

But how, it may well be asked at this point, has such an approach to public policy managed to survive into the age of modern political parties and modern cabinet government? Even in de Geer's day it embodied a strong element of political myth. For de Geer himself represented a well-defined political position, hoping as he did that effective discussion about public policy might be restricted to the propertied and to the educated minority. The cameral reform which he sponsored, moreover, served rather to increase the bitterness of faction than to diminish it and did nothing to realize the ideal of achieving steady "straight-line" political advance with the minimum of oscillation. If there was, then, an element of myth about this approach in de Geer's time, one might suspect that under present-day conditions the element of myth has increased to the point at which the whole tradition serves simply to disguise the facts.

This, however, is decidedly not the case: the spirit of *saklighet* still colours Swedish political activity in a distinctive way. In part this is a question of the survival of institutional devices and procedures. The sending out of draft legislation by government departments on remiss still occurs to administrative agencies with expertise in the subject-matter concerned. The style of any subsequent public exchanges on points of detail is very much affected by the spirit of *saklighet*. Consultation has, moreover, been extended as of right in this field to the giant organizations which have grown up (as so many commentators have noted) to represent employers, manual workers, white-collar workers, farmers, local government authority associations, etc. The representatives of these organizations at national level trade with the Government with authority in their own right—the growth of "Harpsund democracy" was noted earlier—and they have increasingly come to be allotted administrative functions as "laymen": it is a nice question whether or not they might be better classified as a new kind of expert.

Government departments, as has been seen, show an almost Platonic care in setting out the rationale of, and the background to, government propositions. To read these and also the reports of commissions of inquiry, one might almost suppose that the spirit of *saklighet* rules all, and that it is the spirit of party which is the myth. The meticulous documentation is intended for the benefit of interested bodies, in particular for the parliamentary standing committees. Certainly it is true that a good many points of legislative detail are dealt with in standing committee *after* the political parties have decided their attitude to them in private conclave. But the point is here that the system opens the way to a relatively generous degree of accommodation on lesser points; permits the opposition groups a relatively generous right of effective initiative within well-defined limits; and puts a premium on the arguing through of cases on their merits. This holds good both of the parliamentary standing committees, which will continue even after the unicameral reform to be small enclaves of men mostly long mutually acquainted, and of the commissions of inquiry, many of whose members are also often mutually acquainted.

The traditions of the Riksdag, again, discourage displays of passionate advocacy or of partisan zeal. The ruling conventions favour the cool, matter-of-fact presentation of cases. In between election times, the conference of party leaders is occasionally employed for the discussion of some nationally important question of policy.

At this point the analysis comes close to Stjernquist's study of the nature of the opposition in the Swedish political system.[1] In between elections, Stjernquist argues, the opposition seeks a share in policy-making proportionate to its strength (the more so because of the long-term effects of modern policy planning); as election time draws near, the opposition groups approximate more closely to the classical model of opposition behaviour and bend their energies to getting the Government out. The survival of institutional devices and procedures favourable to the continued influence of the spirit of *saklighet* assumes obvious additional importance in the light of the attitude of opposition groups to their role in the periods between elections. The post-war revival of the idea of a national coalition is also relevant here.

The forthcoming unicameral reform will bring with it an increase in the frequency of general elections in Sweden—once every three years instead of once every four, as hitherto. Logically, therefore, we may expect to see something of a decrease in the influence of the spirit of *saklighet* on Swedish political life. But the institutional and procedural arrangements outlined above will persist largely unchanged and seem likely to work in the same direction as before.

The second characteristic of the Swedish political style may now be briefly considered, namely the radical rationalist spirit. Perhaps this particular characteristic is not so distinctive as that which has just been discussed: something of the same spirit, it may be argued, can be observed in the Britain of the 1960's, where political institutions are also undergoing a measure of reshaping. Nevertheless there are some interesting aspects of the Swedish situation which are worth a closer look.

In the first place, a radical rationalist spirit is, in the nature of the case, hostile to tradition and to the unquestioning acceptance of inherited ways of doing things. In the Swedish instance, the existence of a set of basic laws which had obviously become obsolescent in many respects can be said to have acted as a catalyst in the matter of institutional reform. The terms of reference of the original Commission on the Constitution of the 1950's, as has been seen, broadened out the inquiry beyond a study of the particular areas where the

[1] In Dahl, *op. cit.*, pp. 116–46.

shoe was pinching and turned it into a "comprehensive review of the working problems of democracy". An unsentimental root-and-branch study of the entire range of Swedish political institutions was thus inaugurated and, as has also been seen, is still working itself out.

Secondly, modern technological and big business methods made a relatively early impact on Swedish government and administration. For most of the post-war period there has been a preoccupation with rationalization studies and (more recently) with cost–benefit analysis. During this period the Swedish industrial and business world has adopted many of the attitudes of its American counterparts (without, of course, being able to operate on the same scale). It may also be added here that Sweden has long enjoyed something of a reputation for producing economic analysts and that there has been a steady inflow into the administration of people highly qualified in this sphere.

Thirdly, and connected with this last point, the rise of the social sciences generally (in Sweden as elsewhere) has led to the rise of the administrator with a more comprehensive interest than hitherto in what is often called "social engineering". Frequently, though not invariably and not necessarily, the inclination of this new type of administrator is to regard existing arrangements with a critical and far-ranging eye. On balance it seems fair to say that in the Swedish case the radical rationalist spirit has derived some accession of strength from this quarter.[2]

Fourthly, as was mentioned at an earlier stage of this book, the centre of gravity of the Swedish electorate has now been left of centre for a considerable time. Developments before 1939 no doubt helped to pave the way for this. In 1936 Ohlin, for the Liberal Party, combined the party's traditional support for the defence of private enterprise and of a wide measure of economic freedom with support for an active social welfare policy and for measures of state intervention and planning in the economic sphere (chiefly to promote and maintain full employment). This was formulated as

[2] This spirit is expressed with singular clarity, for example, in Wickman and Pålsson's article, Ideologisk upplösning och förnyelse, in *Tiden*, 1948, pp. 152–62.

"social liberalism". The pre-1939 co-operation between Agrarians and Social Democrats has already been noted, as has also its post-war recurrence: the Centre Party has, on the whole, continued to show itself the most sympathetic to the Social Democrats of all the opposition groups. At the same time a strong current of egalitarianism can be discerned in the Liberal Party's post-war line. Thus we find, e.g. in the 1962 Liberal programme statements supporting the abolition of class differences; calling for increased influence and responsibility to be given to employees (a familiar line); urging equality for theoretical and practical education in schools; and affirming that all work has the same social value. A radical rationalist strain, it can be said, ran through liberalism in Sweden even before the formation of a Liberal Party: freethinkers and dissenters provided the component strands.

Various commentators have remarked on a period of convergence between party positions in Sweden, drawing attention, for example, to the general acceptance that has been gained for the principles of the welfare state. Recently, as was argued earlier in this work, inter-party divisions—at least, as between the government side and the opposition side—have been sharpening again. Is this to be attributed to the present election-dominated phase of Swedish politics, or are there deeper underlying forces at work? These are as yet uncharted waters, but there does appear to be the distinct possibility of a wider long-term divergence between Government and Opposition. Polarization would be likely to occur with an increase in ideological commitment and influence on the part of the younger generation radicals within the Social Democratic Party. Apart from that, any movement towards income uniformity, for example, would be likely to cut across the widely held opposition belief in the value of monetary incentives. It seems highly doubtful whether the Liberal view that "all work has the same social value" is to be interpreted as meaning that it should have the same financial reward.

Signs of an older, populist type of radicalism can be observed in the Centre Party and, to a lesser extent, the Liberal Party. These reflect a malaise in face of increasing concentrations of economic and political power and in face of what is felt to be the increasing authority of the expert. Thus the Centre Party lays stress on the role of education in closing the gap between the expert and the citizen, and both parties have strong currents of opinion running in favour of strengthening grass-roots democracy as an antidote to the large impersonal structures increasingly characteristic of contemporary social life.

Against this background it may be of interest to conclude this survey with a note outlining some of the suggestions for reform that have been broached of late in the provincial government sector.

PROVINCIAL GOVERNMENT REFORM

The desire for more coherent planning is a powerful factor making for change at the provincial government level, as elsewhere in the administration. Ever since the time of Gustavus Adolphus, the central government has wielded authority over the localities through the agency of the provincial governments (*länsstyrelser*)—branches of the central administration having the status of central boards. The pattern of twenty-four provinces plus the city of Stockholm survived unchanged from the early nineteenth century until last year, when a first change was made. It has come under heavy and increasing criticism as being too fragmented to provide the resources required for, for example, efficient hospital administration, traffic control, and regional economic planning. The arrival of the computer has increased the pressure for larger-scale administrative units so as to reap the advantages of the speedy processing of masses of routine data. Moreover the difficulties in the way of co-ordination have been compounded by the growth at provincial level, notably during the 1940's, of offshoots of specialized central boards such as the Highways and Waterways Board (now the State Highways Board) or the Labour Market Board.

These considerations have led to the appointment during the past 7 or 8 years of a whole series of commissions of inquiry into various aspects of government at provincial level. The first major reform to result from the deliberations of these commissions was the amalgamation of the city and the province of Stockholm in January 1968. A drastic overhaul of boundary lines elsewhere seems likely to follow the report, in May 1967, of the inquiry set up some 4 years earlier to investigate the subject. The recommendations, if accepted, would involve the reduction of the total number of provinces to fifteen and the redrawing of boundaries to such an extent that only three of the existing units would survive intact. Another commission of inquiry, reporting at the same time, has proposed that various officials serving the specialized boards at provincial level should be incorporated into the provincial governments in the interests of closer co-ordination. It has also urged that the provincial governments themselves should to some extent be politicized.

This last point is worth a closer look. At the moment provincial governments are staffed by civil servants under the leadership of a provincial governor who is appointed by the central government and who, as was seen earlier, is often, though by no means invariably, an ex-politician. The Commission proposes that the Provincial Governor should preside over a board of ten which shall be answerable to the Provincial Council for the running of the province. Six of these ten would be elected by the Provincial Council, the other four would be chosen by the central government. A strong minority on the Commission—4 out of 9—would have all ten members of the board elected by the Provincial Council. In either event the board would be composed of politicians. Provincial councils, it should be added, are elective bodies which have been in existence for over a century. They have their own executive committees, usually chosen on a proportional representation basis, to supervise the administration of their services. The proposed new arrangements would mean an expansion of the responsibilities of politicians at the provincial level.

The projected reform may be seen in part as one aspect of a much wider movement which has set in with particular force during this last decade: the movement to bring the administrative system into closer touch with the public it is designed to serve by injecting into it "lay" representatives, often at a high level. Sometimes these lay representatives are politicians, sometimes they represent interest groups and sometimes they are simply citizens with a particular expertise relevant to the task in hand. Of course it is true that persons in all three categories have been linked in with the administrative system at various levels for many years past. But of late—as was mentioned earlier in this book—the process has become much more noticeable, the reflection of a conscious policy. Thus the governing boards of the great trading agencies were converted from civil service to lay boards in 1962; a variety of other boards have been reconstituted along similar lines, as, for instance, the State Highways Board (1966) and the Social Welfare Board (1968); and new boards have been created according to the same principle, such as the Police Board (1965) and the State Traffic Safety Board (1968). At the same time there has been a marked tendency to strengthen the element of lay representation on specialized administrative agencies at provincial level—provincial school boards, for example.

The trend towards larger-scale provinces has been accompanied by a certain amount of agitation for reconstituting provincial governments so as to allow greater variety in regional administration and greater independence of Stockholm. The proposals outlined above for politicizing provincial governments may be seen as a modest bow in this direction: the minority report advocates a longer step along the same road. Private members' motions tabled during the parliamentary sessions of 1963 and 1964 called for the setting up of regional parliaments, governments, and Ombudsmen and led to discussions about whether or not provincial governors should be converted into regional premiers responsible to their respective provincial councils. To some extent this agitation represents a reaction against what is felt to be the impersonality, remoteness, and uniformity of the large-scale unit, to some extent it has a political motivation. It does not appear likely to make a great deal of headway in the last-mentioned version above, but the general movement has a considerable head of steam behind it and it will be interesting to see what happens. The latest report in this field—the inquiry into democracy at provincial government level—recommended *inter alia* (in November 1968) that the elective provincial councils (*landsting*) should handle the work of regional planning and co-ordination among other business transferred from the provincial governments. It also suggested that these same provincial councils should appoint a majority of "lay" members to serve on the specialized state administrative committees, etc., at provincial level. The extension of lay representation within the administrative system is in part, of course, an attempt to deal with the complaint of remoteness. Grants of autonomy to the regions are, however, likely to be circumscribed by the demands of economic planning and by the fear of distortions induced by sectional pressures.

Enough has been said to illustrate the thoroughness and determination with which the Swedes have recently set about overhauling their political system. If in certain sectors the rate of change has been sedate, the explanation lies in the desire to achieve the maximum of agreement. It is towards this end that the machinery for evolving reforms in Sweden traditionally grinds both slow and small

Bibliography

Note: *The Swedish letters Å, Ä and Ö are classed as A and O in this list.*

ALBINSSON, G., and ELANDER, K., *Våra landsting*, Liber, Stockholm, 1964.

ALEXANDERSON, N., *Justitieombudsmannen, Militieombudsmannen, Tryckfrihetskommittén*, Sveriges Riksdag, Vol. 16, Petterson, Stockholm, 1935.

ANDERSSON, G., *Vem gör vad i länen*, Landskommunernas förbund, Stockholm, 1959.

ANDERSSON, I., *et al.*, *Författningsreform—nytt alternativ*, Tiden, Stockholm, 1963.

ANDRÉN, G., *et al.*, *Sveriges styrelse*, Petterson, Stockholm, 1937.

ANDRÉN, N., *Från kungavälde till folkstyre*, Ehlins, Stockholm, 1955.

ANDRÉN, N., *Modern Swedish Government*, Almqvist & Wiksell, Stockholm, 1961.

ANDRÉN, N., *et al.*, *Svensk statsförvaltning i omdaning*, Almqvist & Wiksell, Uppsala, 1965.

ARNESON, B. A., *The Democratic Monarchies of Scandinavia*, 2nd edn., Van Nostrand, New York, 1949.

BEXELIUS, A., *The Swedish Institution of the Justitieombudsman*, Swedish Institute, Stockholm (Reprint from *The International Review of Administrative Sciences*, 1961, No. 3; published by the International Institute of Administrative Sciences, Brussels).

BOHEMAN, E., *På Vakt*, Norstedt Stockholm, 1964.

BRUSEWITZ, A., *Riksdagen och utrikespolitiken*, Statsrådets ansvarighet, Sveriges Riksdag, Vol. 15, Petterson, Stockholm, 1938.

CHAPMAN, B., *The Profession of Government*, Allen & Unwin, London, 1959.

Constitution of Sweden, The, Royal Ministry of Foreign Affairs, in English (translation by S. Thorelli), Stockholm, 1954.

CRONER, F., *Tjänstemannakåren i det moderna samhället*, Almqvist & Wiksell, Uppsala, 1951.

ELDER, N. C. M., The parliamentary role of joint standing committees in Sweden, *American Political Science Review*, 1951, pp. 464–73.

ELDER, N. C. M., Parliament and foreign policy in Sweden, *Political Studies*, 1953, pp. 193–206.

ELDER, N. C. M., The Swedish election of 1956, *Political Studies*, February 1957, pp. 65–78.

ELDER, N. C. M., Swedish constitutional reform proposals, 1963, *Parliamentary Affairs*, Summer, 1963, pp. 302–7.

FAHLBECK, E., *Tryckfrihetsförordningen 1949*. Studier tillägnade Fredrik Lagerroth, Gleerup, Lund, 1950, pp. 130–54.

FOYER, L., *Former för kontakt och samverkan mellan staten och organisationerna*, Stockholm, 1961 (reprinted from SOU, 1961: 21).

GOVERNMENT PROPOSITIONS: 1956: 161, Ombudsman.
1957: 86, Legal and social science training.
1957: 150, Local government reform.
1958: 31 and 157, Civil Service pension rights.
1960: 126, O & M reorganization.
1961: 180, Local government reform.
1964: 48, Social Science course overhaul.
1964: 100 and 101, Nationalization of police.
1964: 163, Local government reform.
1965: 42, O & M reorganization.
1965: 60, Reform of civil service right of collective bargaining.
1965: 65, Chancery reform.

GRANSTRÖM, K. O., *Länsdemokrati och regional Samhällsplanering*, Tiden, 1965, pp. 140–6.

GRÜNTHAL, T., *Modern kommunförvaltning*, 2nd edn., Bonniers, Stockholm, 1965.

HÅSTAD, E., *Partierna i regering och riksdag*, 2nd edn., Bonniers, Stockholm, 1949.

HÅSTAD, E., *The Parliament of Sweden*, Hansard Society, London, 1957.

HECKSCHER, G., Konselj och statsrådsberedning, *Statsvetenskaplig Tidskrift*, 1948, pp. 305–15.

HECKSCHER, G., *Decentraliseringsproblemet inom statsförvaltningen*, Studier tillägnade Fredrik Lagerroth, Gleerup, Lund, 1950, pp. 155–71.

HECKSCHER, G., *Staten och organisationerna*, 2nd edn., Ko-operativa förbundet, Stockholm, 1951.

HECKSCHER, G., *Svensk statsförvaltning i arbete*, 2nd edn., Norstedt, Stockholm, 1958.

HERLITZ, N., *Sweden: A Modern Democracy on Ancient Foundations*, University of Minnesota Press, Minneapolis, 1939.

HERLITZ, N., Den offentliga förvaltningens organisation, *Föreläsningar i förvaltningsrätt*, II, 2nd edn., Norstedt, Stockholm, 1948.

HERLITZ, N., Förvaltningsrättsliga plikter, *Föreläsningar i förvaltningsrätt*, III, Norstedt, Stockholm, 1949.

HERLITZ, N., *Grunddragen av det svenska statsskickets historia*, 4th edn., Norstedt, Stockholm, 1952.

HERLITZ, N., Publicity of official documents in Sweden, *Public Law*, 1958, pp. 50–69.

HERLITZ, N., Critical points of the rule of law as understood in the Nordic countries, *Civibus et Rei Publicae, Festskrift till Georg Andrén*, Almqvist & Wiksell, Stockholm, 1960, pp. 162–75.

HERLITZ, N., *1969 års regeringsform?*, Norstedt, Stockholm, 1963.

HESSLÉN, G., *Det svenska kommittéväsendet intill år 1905*, Almqvist & Wiksell, Uppsala, 1927.

HESSLÉN, G., Departement och verk, Festkrift till Professor Skytteanus Axel Brusewitz, *Skrifter utgivna av Statsvetenskapliga föreningen i Uppsala*, XII, Almqvist & Wiksell, Uppsala and Stockholm, 1941, pp. 246–63.

HESSLÉN, G., *Den svenska förvaltningen*, 3rd edn., Bonniers, Stockholm, 1956.

HÖJER, K. J., *Den svenska socialpolitiken*, 4th edn., Norstedt, Stockholm, 1956.

HÖÖK, E., *Den offentliga sektorns expansion*, Almqvist & Wiksell, Uppsala, 1962.

HULTQVIST, P., Riksdagsopinionen mot ämbetsmannaintressena, Från representationsreformen till 1880 talets början, *Acta Universitatis Gotoburgensis*, 1954: 5, Gothenburg, 1954.

INGELSON, A., *Officiellt*, Natur och Kultur, Stockholm, 1947.

JARILD, H., and ANDERSSON, N., *Kommunalkunskap*, Ehlins, Stockholm, 1956.

KÄLVESTEN, A.-L., *The Social Structure of Sweden*, Swedish Institute, Stockholm, 1965.

LANDSTRÖM, S.-S., Svenska ämbetsmäns sociala ursprung, *Skrifter utgivna av Statsvetenskapliga föreningen i Uppsala*, XXXIV, Almqvist & Wiksell, Uppsala, 1954.

LINDELL, C.-G., *Hur statsförvaltningen arbetar*, Brevskolan, Stockholm, 1960.

MALMGREN, R., *Sveriges grundlagar*, 6th edn., Norstedt, Stockholm, 1955.

MEIJER, H., *Kommittépolitik och kommittéarbete*, Gleerup, Lund, 1956.

MICHANEK, E., *Swedish Government in Action*, Swedish Institute, Stockholm, 1962.

MOLIN, B., *Swedish party politics: a case study*, *Scandinavian political studies*, Vol. 1, 1966, pp. 45–58.

NORDENSTAM, A., Hur regeringen arbetar, *Statsvetenskaplig Tidskrift*, 1957, pp. 245–56.

Nordisk Kontakt. (Nordic journal published approximately fortnightly during parliamentary sessions).

NYMAN, O., *Parlamentarismen i Sverige*, Ehlins, Stockholm, 1950.

NYMAN, O., Rekryteringen till verkschefsposterna, *Statsvetenskaplig Tidskrift*, 1964, pp. 317–35.

OSTERHOLM, G., *Förvaltnings-Sverige*, Norrtälje, 1955.

PETRÉN, T., *Domstolar, departement och ämbetsverk*, Rabén och Sjögren, Ystad, 1962.

RIDLEY, F. F. (ed)., *Specialists and Generalists*, Allen & Unwin, London, 1968.

ROWAT, D. C. (ed.), *The Ombudsman, Citizen's Defender*, Allen & Unwin, London, 1965.

RUSTOW, D. A., *The Politics of Compromise*, Princeton University Press, Princeton, NJ, 1955.

SÄRLVIK, B., Political stability and change in the Swedish electorate, *Scandinavian Political Studies*, Vol. 1, 1966, pp. 188–222.

SKÖLD, P. E., and DE LA MOTTE, T., *Kommunalkunskap*, Tiden, Stockholm, 1963.

STATENS OFFENTLIGA UTREDNINGAR: 1953: 15 and 16, Legal and social science training.
1955: 50, The Ombudsman.
1958: 14, Machinery of government.
1963: 16, 17, 18, Constitutional reform.
1963: 64, Provincial Council organization.
1964: 27, Administration appeals, etc.
1964: 38; 1965: 2, 3, 34, 37, Comments on constitutional reform proposals.
1965: 9 Labour market policy.

STJERNQUIST, N., Nutida budgetprinciper och grundlagens, *Civibus et Rei Publicae, Festskrift till Georg Andrén*, Almqvist & Wiksell, Stockholm, 1960, pp. 444–71.

STJERNQUIST, N., Sweden: stability or deadlock? in Robert A. Dahl, *Political opposition in Western Democracies*, pp. 116–46, Yale University Press, 1966.

STRÖMBERG, H., *Allmän förvaltningsrätt*, Gleerup, Lund, 1962.

SUNDBERG, H. G. F., *Allmän förvaltningsrätt*, Norstedt, Stockholm, 1955. *Sveriges Statskalender* (annual).

TINGSTEN, H., *Skall kungamakten stärkas?*, Bonniers, Stockholm, 1964.

VERNEY, D. V., *Parliamentary Reform in Sweden*, Oxford University Press, Oxford, 1957.

VERNEY, D. V., *Public Enterprise in Sweden*, Liverpool University Press, 1959.

VINDE, PIERRE, *Hur Sverige styres*, Bokförlaget Prisma, Stockholm, 1968.

WALLIN, G., *et al.* (ed.), *Kommunerna i förvandling*, Almqvist & Wiksell, Uppsala, 1966.

WHYATT REPORT, *The Citizen and the Administration*, Stevens, London, 1961.

WICKLÉUS, J.-A., Föredragnings—och beslutsformer inom arbetsmarknadsstyrelsens styrelse, unpublished essay prepared for political science dissertation in Stockholm University, Spring, 1963.

WICKMAN, K., *Vägen till planhushållning*, Tiden, 1951, pp. 270–5.

WICKMAN, K., and PÅLSSON, R., *Ideologisk upplösning och förnyelse*, Tiden, 1958, pp. 152–62.

ZWEIGBERGK, O. VON, *Svensk politik 1905–1929*, Bonniers, Stockholm, 1929.

Index